STD
BUS

EXECUTIVE EMPLOYMENT AND COMPENSATION

EXECUTIVE EMPLOYMENT AND COMPENSATION

The Indispensable Book for CEOs, Directors and Senior Management

Arnold S. Ross

James E. McKinney

Charlotte P. Armstrong

HIRSCHFELD, STERN, MOYER & ROSS, INC.
NEW YORK, NEW YORK

Published by
Hirschfeld, Stern, Moyer & Ross, Inc.,
1270 Avenue of the Americas,
New York, New York 10020

Produced by Spencer Publishing
Enterprises, Los Angeles
Cover and interior page design
by Fred Fehlau

ISBN 0-9631675-1-0

Library of Congress
Catalog No. 92-075362

ACKNOWLEDGMENT

*This book could not
have been produced without
the organizational skills,
editorial assistance, patience
and word-processing proficiency
of Susan Peltz St. John.*

CONTENTS

FOREWORD

⁓

WHY THIS BOOK—and why now? Our 50 years' collective experience as business advisors to boards of directors and board compensation committees, and as personal counselors to senior executives on employment and compensation arrangements, is a significant milestone. It affords an appropriate occasion to reflect on what our experience has taught us, both about the substance of these arrangements and the process for arriving at them.

As to substance, we have learned what is right about executive employment and compensation arrangements and also what is wrong about many of them. These are useful insights, because getting the arrangements right is no harder than getting them wrong. In fact, it really is easier to get them right and especially important over the long term to do so.

Also as to substance, this book is different and it may be unique. Most books consider executive compensation only—whether it is too much or too little, and the forms in which it is paid. This book, reflecting our consulting approach, views employment arrangements as part of a totality, integrating compensation with the executive's long-term financial plan and estate plan.

As to process, we strongly believe that it is a key factor in helping the executive and the employer get to "yes" and a major determinant of any successful substantive outcome. Because process very much shapes the result, it is essential to get it right too. This book is unique in that it addresses the role of process in designing successful employment and compensation arrangements.

For these reasons, we have interwoven considerations of process throughout our examination of the several elements that comprise the employment and compensation arrangements. Each element is the subject of a separate chapter and is discussed from the perspective of the executive and the employer—to identify their respective concerns and viewpoints and to suggest the balancing of interests that is the objective of the process. More often than not, the employer's perspective will represent the realities of the 1990s by providing the framework for negotiations and defining the substantive boundaries.

A final word about process: It requires the building of a relationship that will outlive the negotiation at hand with the individual or individuals who play the key roles of personal counselor to the executive and compensation advisor to the employer. This is to make sure that the arrangements are properly implemented and that they continue to work as contemplated for both parties or are modified to accommodate changed personal or business circumstances.

Notwithstanding these considerations, this book would probably not have been written without the impetus of all that seemed wrong with senior executive compensation in the tumultuous 1980s. The frequent imbalance between pay and performance and the extraordinary excesses of the decade put into sharp relief the irresponsible departure of many companies from the basic principle of pay for performance.

The 1990s are already proving to be markedly different. There has been a "sea change" from what was predominantly a seller's market to more of a buyer's market. Executives are more reluctant to press up-front demands, and boards of directors and compensation committees seem to be more cognizant of their responsibilities to shareholders. In the new environment of leaner corporate staffs and budgets, higher standards of performance and greater accountability, this book imparts an important message of what will, and will not, work in the 1990s.

The book focuses on the employment and compensation arrangements of chief executive officers—with the knowledge that their position in the company is unique. CEOs are different from other executives and, accordingly, should be treated differently. It is they primarily who mold the companies they head. The position of CEO should not be a sinecure; rather, it should be the ultimate risk position and should be rewarded accordingly.

The top of the pyramid necessarily comes first, which means that the CEO's arrangements must be settled before those of the other senior executives can be addressed. The CEO's arrangements establish the boundaries and they help to shape, though do not determine, the arrangements of the other executives.

As the 1980s ended and the United States began to sink into recession, executive pay continued to rise. Indeed, from 1989 to 1990 the median increase in the compensation of the highest-paid executive at 350 of the nation's largest companies was 6.77%. During the same period, shareholder value (share price plus dividends) fell by 9%. In today's climate, this divergent result is no longer acceptable.

While high compensation is not unreasonable in itself, we enthusiastically endorse the new imperative of the 1990s: Pay must be an effective incentive, and it must reward not effort but performance; high pay is justified only when the executive produces superior returns for shareholders. Companies can rightly pay more to get more, but not to stay even or to get less. In other words, pay must be driven by the bottom line and not the top line.

Arnold S. Ross
James E. McKinney
Charlotte P. Armstrong
New York, New York

EXPLANATION OF TERMS

Company
The entity, usually a publicly held corporation, employing the Executive.

Executive/CEO
The chief executive officer of the Company. The discussion concerning the Executive may also apply to other high-level executives. Typically, the Executive will be the chairman of the board of directors of the Company.

Employer
The board of directors of the Company. The term also includes the compensation committee of the board of directors.

THE PROCESS

⌒

THE "PROCESS" of designing, implementing and monitoring executive employment arrangements is a major determinant of the substantive result. Sound process will yield a superior result, unsound process an inferior result.

Too often, though, the Executive and the Company do not give any thought to process; process is revealed, if at all, in retrospect and understood only after the fact—usually in terms of pitfalls that could have been avoided. Thus, process may devolve from lack of leadership rather than evolve through planning and coordination. When properly conceived and adhered to by the parties, process is critical to attaining the desired result—the careful balancing of interests and the structured relationship that will benefit both the Executive and the Company and its shareholders.

Although it need not be, the process for achieving the optimum outcome is often a long one. Not surprisingly, without an agreed process, negotiations can take even longer and still not succeed. Essential to its success—beyond the strong leadership of the individual who will head and coordinate the process—are the early and continuing involvement of the other players, and full and open communication with them at every stage and among them as appropriate.

Also essential is a close understanding of the Company—its corporate culture and style, strategic and business objectives and compensation philosophy. All of these considerations inform the process and help to direct it toward a reasoned result that links pay with performance, executive wealth with shareholder wealth.

The process must build from two directions: the needs of the Executive and the requirements and inherent limitations of the Company. It requires looking into the future and then, in a sense, backing up to make that future a reality for the Executive and the Company.

The endgame of the process is the meeting of minds between the Executive and the Company—the mutually agreed employment and compensation arrangements that are hammered out. Getting to that point is not easy, though, nor should it be.

The Executive is making a mid-career change, often a momentous change, that may define the rest of his or her life—and estate plan as well. In effect, the Executive is walking through a new door into a different world. So, also, is the Company, as selection of the Executive can be a "make-or-break" decision in terms of prospects for the business, without any assurance that the individual will perform as expected.

Typically, the process begins with a Company's need to fill the position of CEO. It can also begin with a Company's decision to undertake a review and evaluation of an *existing* CEO's employment and compensation arrangements. This will increasingly be the case as the SEC's 1992 disclosure rules focus greater attention on executive compensation.

If the position of the CEO is filled from inside the Company, the process will tend to follow a pattern already in place. If an outsider is recruited, the process will start with a clean slate.

In the case of a new CEO—regardless of whether the Company expects to fill the position from the "inside" or the "outside"—a professional recruiter will frequently be involved. When involved, a recruiter may play several roles over the course of time or even simultaneously:

- counseling the Company in setting the specifications for the position to be filled and determining the type of candidate it needs,
- searching for candidates both inside and outside the Company,
- screening and evaluating candidates, and
- counseling the "short list" of candidates as to how best to present themselves.

This phase of the process is like courtship, with the recruiter playing the role of "marriage broker." Even before the courtship phase ends, though, the recruiter would be well-advised to begin widening the process by involving other professionals.

Whether or not a recruiter is in the picture, once the Executive and the Company have agreed to enter into a long-term relationship, the parties should immediately seek the advice and counsel of a specialist in high-level employment and compensation arrangements. The role of the recruiter, when one is involved, does not normally extend to counsel on the fine points of these arrangements. The recruiter is in a good position, however, to recommend—to the Company and the Executive—skilled professionals in this field.

Ideally, the compensation specialist or other professional tapped by the Company will be an "advisor/counselor"—a person who can play the tandem role of business advisor to the Company and personal counselor to the Executive. An individual with these qualifications is best able to lead the process by which the employment arrangements will be designed and to coordinate the efforts and input of the other players—such as lawyers and investment bankers, as well as the compensation committee of the board of directors of the Company and other board members.

The advisor/counselor is the key player—the central person for resolving competing interests and, more important, the person closest to and most trusted by the Executive. Indeed, the advisor/counselor is in the best position to represent the Executive before the compensation committee and the board of directors and to interact as necessary with the corporate bureaucracy in fashioning the employment-compensation package, especially its innovative features.

The first duty of the advisor/counselor is to determine the Executive's objectives—with regard to position, compensation, security, length of commitment, etc. This may take some time, because the process will force the Executive to define his or her long-term financial objectives and articulate compensation goals for the new position, in terms not only of expected levels but also of expected types and time horizons. Thus, an appropriate threshold question to the Executive is, "At the end of the road, when the employment term is over, where do you want to be?"

The advisor/counselor should explore alternative strategies and scenarios with the Executive in order to set and rank priorities and stake out fall-back positions for negotiations with the Company. When the Executive's "wish list" is complete—and it should almost always be committed to writing—the advisor/counselor will then be in a position to sound out the Company and determine its objectives and priorities for the employment and compensation arrangements of the Executive.

Ascertaining the Company's position on the key points of the contemplated arrangements will require in-depth discussion with members of the board of directors and more particularly with the compensation committee of the board. Appropriate threshold questions to the board and the compensation committee are "What do you want?" and "How much are you willing to pay for it?" The compensation committee has a dual role: It participates in the design of the employment arrangements and it recommends—indeed, advocates—those arrangements to the board. Accordingly, the committee's chairman should be intimately involved in the deliberations and, at a minimum, the other members should be kept fully informed and also involved as appropriate at different stages of the negotiations.

While corporate governance is not the subject of this book, quite clearly the 1990s are going to require more of compensation committees—in terms of leadership, assertiveness, accountability and independence. As they find themselves increasingly on the firing line, compensation committees will need to be better-informed, more vigorous in the assertion and protection of shareholder interests and more insulated from conflict of interest—whether real, potential or perceived. Independence may require not only that compensation committees be differently constituted, but also that they be able to retain their own outside advisors and obtain independent second opinions.

Contact by the advisor/counselor with the Company should usually not involve lower levels of management—except possibly for technical input on such matters as employee benefits, perquisites, existing special executive programs, etc.

Once the bargaining positions of the two sides are known, the advisor/counselor can start to build a bridge between the Company and the Executive. Usually this is best done without face-to-face meetings between the parties, with the advisor/counselor acting as go-between. Indeed, more often than not it is counterproductive for the Executive to be involved in negotiating the arrangements. Eventually, if there is a will on both sides, a way will be found to accommodate the concerns, objectives and priorities of the Company and the Executive. Both sides should anticipate making compromises.

The way is then open for other professionals to provide their expertise in fashioning the final arrangements. These will principally be lawyers. Either the Executive's lawyers or the Company's lawyers must prepare the first draft of the required documents, e.g., the employment agreement, the supplemental retirement agreement (if it is not embodied in the employment agreement), the long-term incentive plan, etc. There is a certain advantage in having the initial drafting responsibility, because the documents will inevitably reflect the point of view of that party. If the Company is paying for the preparation of documents, it will quite rightly insist that its lawyers assume this responsibility.

This does not mean that the Executive's attorneys will not have the opportunity to review the documents. However, if the Company's lawyers have fairly and accurately represented the agreement of the parties, the reviewing lawyers' role should be limited to providing technical comments. The same is true if the Executive's attorneys have the initiating role and the Company's lawyers the reviewing role. In the final analysis, if the advisors for both parties have done their job fairly and well, the attorneys' roles will be easier and the process smoother.

A word of caution: Unless they have specific relevent experience, lawyers should not become overly involved in the economic aspects of the package. Except in unusual cases, design of the financial arrangements is not their expertise and they are not comfortable advising on it. Their input should generally be confined to the legality of the arrangements and to such matters as the definition of cause (*Chapter 8*), due process rights upon termination for cause (*Chapter 8*), noncompetition provisions (*Chapter 9*) and nondisclosure of confidential information (*Chapter 10*).

In the long run, executive employment arrangements are only as viable as the willingness of the parties to abide by them, and that willingness is essentially determined by the perception of both parties that the arrangements are fair and equitable and represent a sensitive balance between corporate and individual needs. The professionals involved in designing, implementing and monitoring the arrangements should strive for this result. They will be better able to achieve it if they regard themselves as a single team while recognizing that the individual players have different skills and viewpoints.

The professionals' greatest contribution may lie in establishing and maintaining clear communication between the Employer and the Executive, each of whom has different needs, interests and perspectives. If each party understands and appreciates the other party's point of view, negotiation will be easier and smoother, and the parties will be more assured of an early conclusion and a successful outcome.

Every employment negotiation is different, as is its process, but various elements are common to *all* executive employment agreements. Each of these common elements is the subject of a subsequent chapter and is discussed from the perspective of the Executive and of the Employer—in the belief that a better understanding of each other's viewpoints and concerns will facilitate the balancing of interests that is the objective of the process.

Understanding of and respect for process are essential to the Executive and the Employer in "getting to *yes*." For this reason, process is an integral part of the discussion that follows.

2

TERM OF EMPLOYMENT

EXECUTIVE EMPLOYMENT agreements generally run from three to five years, although longer terms are not uncommon.

The term is one of three types:
- a fixed term with no provision for renewal,
- a fixed term with provision for automatic renewal for the same period or some shorter period, unless the Executive or the Company gives notice to the other party of intent not to renew the term, and
- a perpetually "evergreening" term, with the term of employment renewing on a monthly or even daily basis.

Typically, Executives favor as long a term of employment as possible. The reasons are simple:
- a desire for long-term security, and
- more generous termination benefits, since ter-

mination benefits (*Chapter 8*) are usually tied to the length of employment.

The best arrangement for the Executive is a term of years renewing on a daily basis, *i.e.*, each day of employment extends the term by one day. In some instances, Executives feel secure enough to do without an employment term—or without a formal arrangement entirely. However, the great majority of executives who attain senior management levels by transfer between employers do have a formal employment arrangement and a stated employment term.

The Employer usually favors a shorter term of employment than the Executive seeks, because it does not wish to commit to a long-term obligation, at least not initially. Equally important, excessively long-term arrangements may not withstand the scrutiny of shareholders, particularly institutional shareholders.

There is usually a middle ground, as the Employer wishes to obtain the services of the desired Executive for at least some period of time, and the Executive wants the position. The middle ground is often an "evergreen" provision: After an initial fixed period of employment, the term of employment will automatically renew for a shorter period or periods unless the Executive gives timely notice that he or she does not want it to continue or the Company gives such notice.

An evergreen provision is fair to both parties when it:

- assures the Executive of a fixed term of employment,
- does not bind the Company to an overly long commitment,
- affords each party periodic opportunities to review the desirability of continuing the employment arrangement, and
- provides the Executive with a "cushion" in the event that his or her employment is terminated without cause.

CHAPTER

3

DUTIES AND
RESPONSIBILITIES

⌒

T HE ESSENCE of any employment arrangement is the exchange of an individual's services for monetary or economic reward.

Particularity in a job description is not so important for an Executive as it is for lower-level executives. At any level, however, it does provide a benchmark for determining whether the individual has been
"constructively" terminated and is, thus, entitled to
termination benefits (*Chapter 8*).

More important, all high-level executives, but
especially an Executive, need flexibility in the definition of the particular position and duties. They also
need time to manage their personal affairs and to en-
gage in a reasonable amount of charitable and community activity that will enhance the image of the
Company.

An example of a company that fosters a high
degree of community service and involvement by executives is Procter & Gamble.

Traditional practice has allowed the CEO and other high-level executives time to serve on the boards of directors of other companies. The Company may or may not consider this practice desirable. Even if it does, it may wish to condition such service upon its prior approval. In some cases, the Executive may insist on the right to continue to be employed by (and even be CEO of) an entity unrelated to the Company—especially when any such entity resulted from a management buy-out in which he or she participated.

Also, depending on the nature of the Company, it may be appropriate for the Executive to be an employee and CEO not only of the Company, but also of one or more of its subsidiaries.

Too much specificity in the position and duties of the Executive is usually not in the Company's best interest, because it may tend to limit the Executive's perceptions of the purpose for which he or she was hired, which is the exercise of overall responsibility for the management and success of the Company.

However, the Employer should seek to maintain some control over the Executive's outside activities. In the case of a newly-hired Executive, a problem may arise concerning existing board memberships. Quite reasonably, the Employer will wish to scrutinize such memberships to make sure that no conflict of interest exists. Indeed, it may require, as a condition of employment, that the Executive resign certain outside positions.

4

COMPENSATION OVERVIEW

C OMPENSATION is a focal point of the CEO's relationship with the Company. From the Company's standpoint, the compensation offered must serve to attract the CEO, and the compensation paid should serve to energize and hold the individual. From the CEO's standpoint, compensation is the measure, however imperfect, and the tangible evidence of success.

If the Company is publicly held, compensation is highly visible, and it is certain to be more visible now as a result of the SEC's 1992 disclosure requirements. Also, it is a likely lightning rod for shareholder objections and public outcry. Indeed, in recent years much shareholder and public attention *has* been paid to executive compensation. This is largely because of the perception—sometimes correct, sometimes not—that the compensation of many CEOs is too high.

To a certain extent, of course, "excessive" compensation is a matter of perception and perspective. On the one hand, a reward to the CEO of 5% of the amount by which shareholder wealth increases on his or her "watch" may not seem excessive. On the other hand, if shareholder wealth increases by $500 million, payment of 5%, or $25 million, to a single individual may seem excessive, if only because the amount is so large. The principle is the same, though, irrespective of the dollars involved. Thus, a reward to a CEO based on an increase in shareholder wealth must take into account the percentage increase as well as the dollar amount.

Several factors have converged to sharpen the perception that CEO compensation is too high: the striking excesses of the 1980s, a recessionary economy, widespread and drastic downsizing of companies, operating losses, negative cash flow, declining real wages, loss of market share, noncompetitiveness, etc. Against this background, senior executive pay has become a national issue.

UNITED STATES VS. FOREIGN COUNTRIES

President Bush's visit to Japan in January 1992, with the CEOs of 12 major U.S. corporations, put a harsh spotlight on the disparity between pay and performance at many of those corporations. It also put a spotlight on the disparity between the compensation of CEOs in the United States and Japan. The average annual compensation of the 12 U.S. CEOs who accompanied President Bush exceeded $2 million in 1990. The average for Japanese CEOs is about one-sixth of that amount—$300,000 to $400,000. Moreover, with Japan's 65% top marginal tax rate, take-home pay is considerably less than that. In other countries, high marginal tax rates are also a factor in lower pay levels.

Another disparity highlighted by President Bush's visit is that between CEO pay and rank-and-file pay in the United States and Japan. American CEOs taken together earn 160 times more than the average worker, whereas Japanese CEOs earn only 16 times more.

Comparisons between CEO pay in the two countries are not entirely valid, however. CEOs in Japan are paid less in part because the directors of corporations there tend to be insiders, with a bias toward limiting the gap in pay with the rank and file. In the United States directors still tend to be the CEOs of other corporations, with a bias that favors high compensation levels. Moreover, the lower pay level in Japan fosters expensive gifts and lavish expense accounts, so that much compensation there is "hidden" in the form of unreported and untaxed perquisites.

More important, though, the disparate compensation standards and practices in the two countries spring from different historical and cultural backgrounds. The Japanese heritage fosters a team approach, which makes it unseemly for pay differentials to be too great. By the same token, Japanese senior executives are expected to take "voluntary" pay cuts when their companies are troubled.

In this regard, it is noteworthy that, in the face of General Motors' $4.5 billion loss in 1991, CEO Robert C. Stempel's 1991 salary of $1 million was down 31% from $1.44 million in 1990. At the Ford Motor Company, which lost nearly $2.3 billion in 1991, CEO Harold A. Poling took a 6.6% pay cut from 1990, earning $1.4 million in salary and bonus in 1991.

In comparison to performance, U.S. executive compensation was still "excessive" by Japanese standards (as well as by sound U.S. standards), and there is no evidence that the pay cuts that did occur were voluntary. However, the reductions do at least bespeak some recognition of the troubled times that had befallen these companies.

In contrast to Japan and other countries, the United States has always been the land of the entrepreneur and free-wheeling individualist—where "the sky is the limit." Foreigners are often said to emigrate to this country for political freedom. An equal, if not more important, reason is the almost complete *economic* freedom they find here. In the United States, free-market forces rule to a greater degree than anywhere else in the world. Consequently, executive compensation levels are higher here than in countries that have a tradition of state capitalism, government control and a less open society.

Reflecting this entrepreneurial bias, compensation in the United States, particularly at the CEO level, includes substantially more incentive compensation than elsewhere. In the United States, incentive compensation (which typically includes an equity-appreciation opportunity) is large enough to make total pay dwarf that in other countries—even taking into account the value of untaxed perquisites and higher executive retirement benefits in those countries.

Many of the most highly compensated executives of public companies in the United States are "mature entrepreneurs"—two classic examples being William H. Gates of Microsoft Corporation and Leon C. Hirsch of U.S. Surgical Corporation. To a great extent, any company seeking entrepreneurial talent at the CEO level must offer a compensation package competitive with what the executive might achieve on his or her own.

With the growth of political freedom throughout the world has come a dramatic growth in economic freedom. Newly liberated or newly formed countries are following America's lead and are likely to do so in executive compensation as in other economic practices. Predictably, the United States will set the standard that others will seek to emulate and adapt to their special circumstances.

Moreover, with the increasing internationalization of economies and the increasing globalization of trade, competition for competent executives will escalate. The same forces that drew scientists and other special talents to the United States a few decades ago will either attract executives from abroad to our shores or lead these same individuals to insist on compensation at home comparable to what they could receive in the United States (Fig. 1).

This is not to argue that executive compensation practices in the United States are without fault. Certainly not! It is to state, however, that such practices are more likely than not to prevail and proliferate internationally. Even as America is a beacon for democracy, so also will it become a bellwether for executive compensation abroad. Thus, it is more important than ever that our compensation practices be properly grounded and structured.

CORPORTATE GOVERNANCE REFORM

The attack on executive compensation is against a background of mounting concern over corporate governance—how corporations manage their affairs for the benefit of shareholders and how they discharge their accountability and responsibility to shareholders. This concern has been spurred by institutional investors and other activists, who bring pressure to bear on companies they have targeted as "underperforming." Among the companies recently under attack on this ground are Sears, Roebuck & Company, Westinghouse Electric Corporation and

FIGURE I

TOTAL 1991 REMUNERATION

CHIEF EXECUTIVE OFFICERS OF COMPANIES

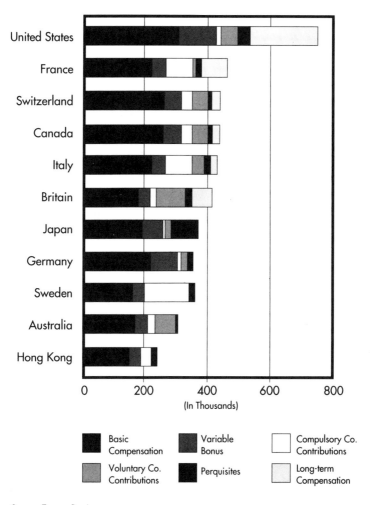

(In Thousands)

Basic Compensation

Variable Bonus

Compulsory Co. Contributions

Voluntary Co. Contributions

Perquisites

Long-term Compensation

Source: Towers Perrin

American Express Company.

For example, in 1991, in the wake of ITT Corporation's poor performance, the California Public Employees Retirement System challenged ITT on CEO Rand Araskog's compensation (between $7 million and $11.5 million for 1990, depending on how it is measured). As a result, his arrangements were modified and ITT announced that it would change the way it compensates senior executives to link pay more closely to performance. Responding to similar pressure concerning CEO Stephen M. Wolf's 1990 compensation, UAL Corporation announced that it would in future make fuller and clearer proxy disclosure of the different elements of executive compensation and the bases for determining them.

In an earlier era, the solution to underperformance was passive—sell one's stock in the company and invest the proceeds elsewhere. In the 1980s, the solution was corporate restructuring via an outside takeover, typically a leveraged buyout. In the 1990s, the emerging solution is corporate restructuring via board of directors reform (aided typically by outside pressure), an "inside" takeover. The result—as evidenced most vividly in the resignation of Robert C. Stempel as chairman and CEO of General Motors—promises to be a parade of departing CEOs and other senior executives in favor of new blood deemed better able to serve the interests of companies and their shareholders.

Board reform is finding expression in various

measures as institutional investors press for change and openness in order to improve performance and enhance accountability. One such measure is to split the roles of board chairman and CEO. While approximately 20% of major American corporations divide the position between two individuals, currently no more than 5% assign the chairmanship to an *independent* director rather than an insider who has retired as an active employee.

However, many corporations are expected to follow the example of General Motors in naming an outside director—John G. Smale—as chairman. IBM Corporation has been mentioned as one such. Indeed, the British have long adhered to the practice—in their parlance—of a "nonexecutive chairman." It avoids the inherent conflict of interest when a CEO chairs the board of a company to which he or she also reports as an employee.

Other corporate governance measures are finding their way into shareholder resolutions in the proxy statements of companies that institutional investors have targeted as underperformers. These include proposals for (1) a board with a majority of independent directors, (2) annual election of all directors, (3) a committee of independent directors to nominate new board members, (4) limitation on directors' terms, (5) a compensation committee comprised only of independent directors and (6) confidential proxy voting. The SEC's 1992 proxy disclosure rules make another gesture toward openness by allowing shareholders to communicate with one another and with management about corporate policy and by encouraging management to seek out shareholders' views.

Another remedial measure, which boards of directors or compensation committees are adopting on their own initiative, is to retain an independent compensation consultant to conduct a review or "audit" of the executive compensation program. Such a review is analogous to a medical "second opinion." It can serve as an external check to confirm the appropriateness of proposed or existing arrangements, or it can help to resolve disagreement concerning a program and identify an alternative course. In either case, the emerging use of audits underscores the shift of control in compensation matters from management to the board of directors.

FEDERAL AND FINANCIAL ACCOUNTING STANDARDS BOARD MOVES

If these pressures were not enough in themselves to force change, more were building up in the public domain as the 90s began. On October 21, 1992, the SEC delivered the *coup de grace* with its new proxy disclosure rules. Now, not only must each publicly reporting company disclose more specific information on compensation elements than previously, but it must include a value for stock options granted in any year.

Also, the compensation committee must discuss the relationship of the company's performance to the CEO's compensation for the year, describing each measure of performance, whether quantitative or qualitative, on which it based such compensation. Further, it must discuss the company's compensation policies with respect to executive officers generally, including the extent to which compensation is performance-related. Finally, the rules prescribe a stock performance graph comparing the five-year cumulative shareholder return of the company to the return of (1) a broad equity market index and (2) an industry index or a company-selected peer group.

In the legislative arena, bills are sure to be reintroduced in Congress to give shareholders an increasing say over the compensation of high-level executives. Also sure to be reintroduced are proposals to cap the amount of tax-deductible compensation that may be paid to an officer of a corporation in any year.

On still another front, the Financial Accounting Standards Board has reopened the question of charging earnings for option grants. The issue again is the amount of the charge and the time when the charge will be incurred. The Board has tentatively agreed that required disclosure should include (1) the method (such as an option pricing model) used to determine fair value and (2) the weighted average of both the fair value and the exercise price of options granted during the year.

Required public disclosure of high-level executive compensation is one thing; government regulation of pay is quite another. The distortions that regulation produces are amply demonstrated by President Nixon's failed wage and price controls and by the "golden parachute" rules. Whatever weaknesses exist in current executive pay practices can be better remedied by market forces—reinforced by greater public disclosure—than through government intervention.

COMMENTS

With all of these developments in the private and public sectors, it is no surprise that executive compensation—both its substance and its rationale—is a paramount concern in the 1990s. All of the pressures for performance improvement and governance reform converge in this subject. The very term "executive compensation" is pejorative, and public companies are on the defensive, as never before, to explain and justify their practices. No longer is it safe, or even possible, to hide behind the platitudes that frequently passed for a coherent compensation philosophy.

Another emerging difference about the 1990s is that, although substantial compensation may be paid, increasingly it will be because rigorous performance criteria have been met or exceeded. Executives will be expected to assume more of the risk. Emphasis will be less on salary and more on incentive compensation. The rewards, while less certain, will have the potential to be even greater. The structure promises to be more objective and more rational.

In the 90s also, a potentially large compensation package is no guarantee that the amounts will be paid. Only recently, chairman Edward H. Budd, and two other senior executives of The Travelers Corporation agreed to give up their "golden parachutes," apparently as a condition precedent to Primerica Corporation's purchase of 27% of Travelers' stock. Because the investment, although friendly, constituted a "change in control," the executives would have received parachute payments if they then lost their jobs without cause.

If the business goes bad and the executive has failed to perform, not only may payment be withheld but the arrangements themselves may be drastically renegotiated. In a worst-case scenario, a company may even repudiate the arrangements, as Salomon Brothers did when John Gutfreund and three executives were forced to resign in 1991. Salomon stopped paying Gutfreund's office and legal expenses and canceled his health insurance. It also refused to pay him the $12.4 million in severance, bonuses and stock options that he claimed he was entitled to receive.

If the business fails, creditors or regulators may attack large compensation/severance packages, as happened at MNC Financial Inc. and Mutual Benefit Life Insurance Co. Moreover, the company may seek to recover compensation paid, as Drexel Burnham Lambert did in suing Michael Milken for the return of $1 billion in compensation paid to him between 1985 and 1989 and in suing other employees for the return of bonuses. Under the settlement terms of Drexel-related civil suits, Milken will pay $500 million and other former Drexel officials $300 million.

UNIQUENESS OF THE CEO

In the United States it is easy to single out particular companies and individual CEOs for criticism, which many people and organizations have done and will continue to do. It is more difficult and more constructive to concentrate on the principles and precepts that should determine a CEO's compensation and make them work in a particular situation.

The first principle is that no two CEOs are alike—in terms of age, educational and other qualifications, experience, earnings history, etc. So also, no two companies are alike—in terms of size, capital structure, ownership, product line, corporate history and culture, compensation philosophy, etc. For this reason, comparing CEO compensation in a peer group of companies or other competitive universe may not be useful except to establish general guidelines for an appropriate package—both the amount of compensation and the mix of compensation elements.

Defining the "peer group" itself is not easy.

Does it mean, for example, companies in more or less the same line of business, companies of similar size in terms of revenue base or capitalization, companies in the same geographical area or companies with the same pattern of growth? In light of the 1992 SEC disclosure requirement that a company compare its five-year cumulative shareholder return with that of one or more peer-group companies, should it mean any companies selected for this purpose? No matter which definition is chosen, the "fit" will almost certainly not be perfect.

Thus, while a peer-group survey assumes importance in justifying the end result, it must not *dictate* the CEO's compensation. Nevertheless, the Company is properly concerned to "do the right thing," and comparative data can afford some comfort for its decisions and help to buttress the "reasonableness" of a contemplated compensation package. Surveys are useful as a final litmus test, but not as a place to begin, where they tend to impede creative, focused thinking.

What is true for the CEO in this regard is not necessarily true for the other senior executives of the Company. The duties of their positions—*e.g.,* chief operating officer, chief financial officer and vice presidents of marketing, human resources and the like—lend themselves more easily to definition and are more likely to be defined in terms that support comparability with similar positions in peer-group companies. Even here, however, it is important to keep in mind the uniqueness of any high-level management position in a particular company.

It is a given that the Company will have to pay "up" to obtain the services of the CEO who fits its needs. Also, the Company will have to pay more to bring in someone from the outside than to promote from within. More important than the amount of compensation, though, is the structure of the package.

Because the CEO is the "point person," his or her compensation should be predicated on the individual's "game plan" for the Company or vision of what the Company will become. In other words, the CEO's compensation should emerge from, be closely related to and reflect the Company's strategic plan— with earning opportunities tied to achievement of successive milestones in the plan. Adherence to this precept may have the healthy effect of forcing the CEO to develop a strategic plan where one does not exist or to update an existing plan. In order to justify the linkage with compensation, the strategic plan must be sufficiently ambitious to stretch the CEO and challenge other high-level executives of the Company.

A pay package predicated on the achievement of such a strategic plan may ultimately prove very generous if the plan's goals are met, but shareholders should not object in this case, because they stand to benefit correspondingly. By the same token, the Company's compensation committee can feel comfortable in designing and recommending such a package, and the board of directors in approving it.

However, the Company cannot be content simply to implement the strategic plan and the pay package. It must monitor the strategic plan against corporate performance and review the pay package to ensure the maintenance of a proper risk/reward relationship: The object is to reward performance appropriately, and at the same time to ensure that nonperformance is not rewarded, to the detriment of shareholders.

The point that cannot be overemphasized is that for CEOs there are no fixed rules. Consequently, the chapters on compensation that follow make no attempt to quantify CEO compensation. Rather, they describe various forms of compensation generally in use and comment on the appropriateness of each in different situations.

OUTSIDE DIRECTORS' COMPENSATION

Related to, but different from, the compensation of the CEO and other high-level executives is the compensation of outside directors. With executive compensation in the spotlight, directors' compensation is also coming under greater scrutiny—this at a time when reform is sweeping the boardroom and the role of outside directors is being redefined to make them less passive and more active.

Historically, as with executive compensation,

too much of directors' compensation has been "automatic"—in the form of an annual retainer for board membership plus meeting attendance fees. Similarly, too little has been related to the performance of either the director or the company on whose board he or she serves.

The traditional compensation package for outside directors consists primarily of an annual retainer for board membership (and sometimes also committee membership) and fees for board and committee attendance. In recognition of the increased work and responsibility, membership on the audit committee or the compensation committee—especially chairmanship of either committee—is often compensated by an additional retainer. With the enhanced role of the compensation committee mandated by the SEC's 1992 disclosure rules, the compensation for service on this committee may be expected to increase markedly. It may involve a retainer for membership on the committee.

Usually directors also receive some form of stock grant and a variety of fringe benefits, such as a retirement plan, medical benefits and life insurance coverage.

Any discussion of the compensation of outside directors must start from an understanding of their role. What they are *not* is employees. Essentially they are representatives of the shareholders. Accordingly, their interests should be allied with those of the shareholders—in compensation as in other matters.

Reflecting their function, directors' compensation has two distinct components: payment for services rendered to the company and incentive for increasing shareholder wealth. The first is paid in cash, the second, when earned, in stock, the value of which fluctuates with the fortunes of the company.

The issue is not the amount of compensation paid but, as in the case of executive compensation, the forms of compensation and their mix and balance. In fact, while outside directors' compensation is often substantial, in many cases it may be *insufficient* to attract the type of individuals that the new standard of corporate governance will demand. As responsibility and power center increasingly in the board, companies need directors who can set the board's agenda, challenge and goad management, be assertive in their independence and assume the risk that independence requires.

The CEO whose feet are being held to the fire by such an activist board may not have the time (or inclination) to serve on other boards. Indeed, it is quite possible to see developing from today's trends a cadre of directors who are not just outside, but truly *independent* and noninterlocking—individuals whose vocation it is to represent shareholder interests. In this regard, it is noteworthy that the 1992 SEC proxy disclosure rules require disclosure of certain "interlocking" compensation committee relationships.

As to the mix of board compensation, it should be weighted far more toward performance and service actually performed than is currently the case.

However, a trend in this direction is clearly discernible with the steady increase in the number of companies using stock-based compensation, either direct grants of stock or options to purchase stock (Fig. 2). A logical extension of this trend should and will be an emphasis on long-term incentive compensation for directors.

At the same time, companies should give serious consideration to paying *per diem* compensation to directors who perform special services or undertake special tasks for the board. Many directors end up "donating" considerable time to the companies on whose boards they sit. With respect to stock grants, directors should be required to hold the shares they acquire, through direct grant or exercise of options, for the duration of their board service and generally for some period thereafter.

A more controversial component of compensation is the various benefits now being extended to directors by many companies. Typically, these include retirement benefits and various welfare benefits, such as life insurance and medical coverage, and possibly also matching charitable contributions. Such noncash forms of compensation have been perceived as a means of attracting qualified individuals to board service.

However, the indicated benefits are traditionally provided to *employees* and have always been associated with an employment relationship. There is a question, then, of the appropriateness of providing

FIGURE 2

PERCENTAGE OF COMPANIES USING STOCK-BASED COMPENSATION FOR DIRECTORS: 1987-1991

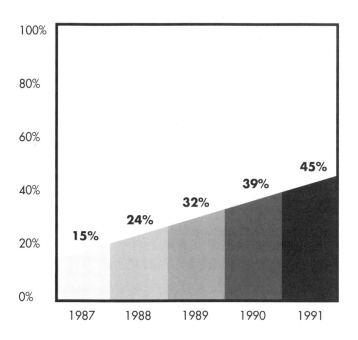

Source: ECRInfo Database of 1,000 Companies

such benefits to board members, whose functions and responsibilities are quite different from those of employees.

The interests of shareholders, which directors are intended to serve, are arguably better served if directors do not receive "employee" benefits. After all, shareholders do not receive retirement or welfare benefits from the corporations in which they hold stock! Moreover, most directors today are already covered by the employee benefit programs of the companies that employ them.

If the day ever comes when "independent director" is a career calling for a large number of people, the provision of benefits can be reexamined in that context. Until that time, there is no valid reason why directors should receive benefits, and corporate resources can be better channeled to other uses—even to incentive compensation for directors.

5

CASH COMPENSATION

C ASH COMPENSATION is the initial
building block of any employment arrangement. However, the higher up the executive
ladder an individual is, the smaller a component of
total compensation it will and should be. Cash compensation falls into two main categories: salary and
bonus.

Because cash is the "king" of compensation—
and, for the five highest-paid officers of a publicly-
traded company, must be disclosed—it is a sensitive
item. While the entitlements of the Executive upon
termination of employment (*Chapter 8*) are also critically important, cash compensation is the central
component of any employment arrangement.

Cash will continue to be central in the 1990s,
but higher individual income tax rates—coupled with
the impact of the SEC's 1992 disclosure rules—may
induce some shift in emphasis from current compensation to deferred compensation.

SALARY

Salary is the keystone of total annual cash compensation. It often forms the benchmark for the balance of the Executive's compensation, particularly when bonuses are expressed as a percentage of salary, and it may be the principal determinant of an Executive's entitlements upon termination of employment.

The relative strength of the bargaining positions of the Executive and the Employer will determine the amount of salary as, indeed, it will determine other terms and conditions of the employment arrangements.

Executives tend to favor compensation that is not "at risk" and thus wish to have salary as high as possible; by the same token, they usually favor automatic raises. Increases in salary can be a fixed percentage or tied to the cost of living or another benchmark, such as the average percentage increase in salary granted the individuals reporting to the Executive. Executives usually favor salary reviews for *increase* only, any such increase to be discretionary with the Employer or based on a review of the Executive's performance or on the achievement of preset goals.

However, Executives should be willing to make concessions on their salary demands in return for the higher rewards they may expect to receive from performance-based compensation. This is particularly true when a new Executive is seeking a higher base salary than the Company has previously paid. The Executive's advisor can often provide a real service to both parties by showing the Executive that it is better to wait for a large "payoff" based on performance than to attempt to get too much money up front.

Quite naturally, the Employer wishes to maintain as much control as it can over the Executive's salary level. Thus, it does not want to be obligated to grant increases, and certainly not automatic increases. These equate with risk avoidance, which should not be a prime characteristic of Executives. The Employer should also have the *right* to decrease salary for poor performance of the Executive.

However, it is unreasonable for the Employer not ever to review the salary of the Executive. Indeed, it is in the Employer's interest to review salary on a regular basis, so that the Executive has a clear evaluation of his or her performance. The customary review period is one year, but there is no reason why it may not be shorter or longer. If the Executive has performed particularly well, the Company can recognize this fact by granting a raise before the end of the normal salary review period. The only caution here is that the Company make clear that it is not setting a precedent for other than regular salary reviews.

If appropriate, the Company should require that salary increases above a certain level be paid in the form of stock options or other stock-based compensation. In 1986, the board of directors of Ralston Purina voted to set the cash compensation of senior management at a level below the average of comparable food companies—in return for "free" shares if the company's stock, then selling at about $60 a share, rose to and held a price above $100 for 10 consecutive trading days. When this finally happened in 1991, William P. Stiritz, CEO, received 160,000 shares, valued at $16.2 million.

An intermediate approach to salary increases, and one that has been adopted by General Mills, allows senior management the choice between cash and stock options.

In any event, the Company should retain the right to "cap" salary—or even total current compensation—if it threatens to get out of proportion or if cash stringencies or other circumstances warrant. In 1990, after the pay of Paul B. Fireman, as CEO of Reebok International, had averaged $13.6 million a year for four years, a new five-year contract capped his annual cash compensation at $2 million: $1 million in salary and up to $1 million in bonus, depending on Reebok's profit performance. In lieu of more cash, he received options to purchase 2.5 million Reebok shares.

In a switch, that might be a portent of the times, James Preston, CEO of Avon Products, recently took the initiative to have an independent review of his current compensation. The result is that he has frozen his salary, at $610,000, and reduced his bonus, from 65% to 50% of an amount tied to Avon's net income and cash flow, in exchange for 50,000 options.

This move was not without precedent, though. In 1989, Anthony Luiso, CEO of International Multifoods, was granted $5 million in options in exchange for his irrevocable waiver of $1 million in compensation to be earned over five years (for the first year, the reduction was $100,000 in salary and $100,000 in bonus; in actuality, he forfeited 10,943 option shares that year, which failed to vest because of a reduced bonus allocation).

Finally, the Company may want to retain the right to reduce salary if performance falls short or losses occur. Thus, as a result of its first annual loss ever in 1991, IBM Corporation reduced the "base pay" (salary and bonus) of John F. Akers, CEO, to $1,175,000, 42% below his 1990 base pay of $2,028,400. Similarly, Westinghouse Electric Corporation reduced the salary of Paul E. Lego, CEO, by $1 million—from $1.6 million in 1990 to $677,083 in 1991—in the wake of a $1.1 billion loss by the company.

BONUS

Bonuses are a customary part of an Executive's compensation. They may be short-term, *i.e.*, paid promptly after the year in which earned, or long-term, *i.e.*, earned and paid over a longer period of time, generally from one to five years. In either case, they need to be in balance with the other components of the package: salary and long-term incentive compensation (if the bonus is long-term, it may take the place of other long-term incentive compensation).

As a general rule, because CEO is the ultimate risk position in the Company, the tilt should be toward at-risk compensation—both short-term and long-term. Thus, it would not be unreasonable for the Company to insist that at least 50% of the Executive's compensation be at risk—as bonus or other incentive compensation or both. By extension, if the bonus is short-term, the bonus opportunity should represent at least 50% of annual compensation.

Bonuses may be categorized as automatic, discretionary or dependent upon performance. Automatic bonuses are generally expressed as a percentage of salary; in effect, they *are* salary—payable usually in a cash lump sum following the close of the year in which earned. Automatic bonuses tend to be paid only in the early years of an Executive's employment, before he or she can have a material effect on the Company's performance. They are a form of "golden hello," discussed below. They are not folded into salary because to do so would inflate salary, and bonuses are customarily treated separately from salary.

When Richard Miller (who had earlier left General Electric) joined Wang Laboratories as CEO, the company guaranteed him three years' salary and bonus totaling $1 million a year.

The award of discretionary bonuses is usually tied to performance. Their advantage is flexibility, *i.e.*, they can be awarded at any time and may be used to send an immediate message that the Executive's efforts and results are recognized.

Performance-based bonuses are payable only upon the achievement of certain preset goals, such as increase in share price, return on equity, earnings per share, etc. They might be of a "target" nature. Richard Ringoen, CEO of Ball Corporation, has a target bonus equal to 65% of his annual salary of $450,000. The payout varies with performance: In any year, he could receive no bonus or a maximum of 135% of salary for exceptional performance.

Payment of short-term bonuses may be deferred at the option of the Executive if the Company has a deferral mechanism in place. The decision whether or not to defer a short-term bonus usually depends on one or more of the following:
- the Executive's cash needs,
- expectations regarding the movement of tax rates, and
- the rate of interest earned on amounts deferred.

Some Executives prefer automatic bonuses. However, with the increasing emphasis on "pay for performance," bonuses—both short-term and long-term—will more likely be discretionary and, then, based on achievement of preset performance goals.

If the bonus is of the performance type, the Executive should have considerable input in setting the performance goals, as he or she is in the best position to influence those goals. The Executive should not push for too easily achieved goals. On the other hand, neither the Executive nor the Employer will be well-served by impossibly high performance goals, the nonachievement of which usually results in mutual frustration.

A self-confident Executive should willingly accept the risk of a performance-based bonus. While a newly hired Executive may not be able to formulate performance goals, provision can be made for setting them after the Executive and the Employer have had the opportunity to review the situation and arrive at reasonably attainable goals. Pending that occasion and before a new Executive has had time to affect the success of the business, he or she should be able to negotiate a guaranteed bonus, but generally not for more than one or two years.

Whatever performance goals define the bonus opportunity, it is essential that the Employer review them periodically, preferably annually, to make certain that they remain valid. It was just such a failure—or maybe inability—of Drexel Burnham Lambert to change its percentage-of-profit bonus formula that resulted in payment of a skewed annual bonus of $550 million to Michael Milken, marking *finis* to the excesses of the 1980s.

A variation of the discretionary or performance bonus is the "transaction" bonus, which an Employer may pay in special circumstances—for example, following a successful acquisition or divestiture. Another variation is a "special" bonus, such as the $10 million bonus paid to J. Hugh Liedtke, chairman of Pennzoil, for "exceptional and extraordinary services" during the company's extended litigation with Texaco.

On occasion an Employer may be willing to pay a sign-on bonus, sometimes referred to as a "golden hello," to obtain the services of a particularly desirable executive. Generally, however, Employers prefer to and should pay bonuses only for superior performance. In this way, using the "stick and carrot," they not only have greater control over cash compensation outlays, but can also expect to secure better performance.

One exception is when the reputation of the Executive is such that his or her association with the Company will be perceived as a benefit—for example, if the Company has been troubled and a particular individual offers the prospect of turning the situation around. This combination of circumstances may explain the very large payment (approximately $15 million) made to Louis V. Gerstner when he signed on as CEO of RJR Nabisco.

Another permissible exception is use of a sign-on bonus to "make up" for bonuses or other payments forfeited by the Executive upon leaving a prior employer. (Gerstner's bonus may have served this purpose in part, too.)

In the few cases when sign-on bonuses may be justified, the Employer should delay payment until the Executive has achieved some, if not all, of the results for which he or she was hired.

6

LONG-TERM INCENTIVE COMPENSATION

~

THE SECOND component of the traditional compensation package of an Executive is long-term incentive compensation. It may take the form of a bonus, but more often is embodied in a separate incentive plan, stock-based or performance-based or a combination of the two. The award is payable either in cash or in stock of the Company, or sometimes in both.

As noted in the discussion of bonuses in *Chapter 5*, a critical issue in the design of an Executive's compensation package is the proper balance among the components: salary, bonus and long-term incentive compensation. "Proper balance" is impossible to define in general terms and has meaning only *vis-a-vis* a specific situation. However, balance involves short-term *versus* long-term compensation and riskless *versus* at-risk compensation. In the 1990s the emphasis will be on at-risk compensation and, increasingly, this will mean long-term incentive compensation.

The trend will accelerate as corporate America—aided by public policy initiatives or otherwise—succeeds in departing from the short-term mind-set of the 1980s.

Generally, as an individual moves up the management ladder, the percentage of compensation at risk increases. For the CEO, it should be at least 50%. The difficult question is how to structure the at-risk component. The structure should be a function of motivation of the Executive, but what motivates? Almost certainly not money alone. Rather, it is the opportunity to set and reach strategic goals and meet quantifiable targets, the achievement of which will translate into money. The incentive opportunity and reward must reflect the challenge of specific goals and targets.

STOCK-BASED INCENTIVE COMPENSATION

Stock is an important and virtually universal component of the incentive portion of the CEO's compensation package. Its significance is as a stake in the long-term growth of the Company.

Stock Options

The most common form of stock-based incentive compensation is the stock option (Fig. 3). The stock

FIGURE 3

TYPES OF STOCK GRANTS
MADE UNDER 185 PLANS
ADOPTED IN 1991

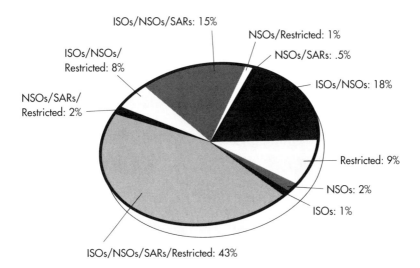

ISOs/NSOs/SARs: 15%

NSOs/Restricted: 1%

ISOs/NSOs/
Restricted: 8%

NSOs/SARs: .5%

ISOs/NSOs: 18%

NSOs/SARs/
Restricted: 2%

Restricted: 9%

NSOs: 2%

ISOs: 1%

ISOs/NSOs/SARs/Restricted: 43%

ISO: Incentive Stock Option
NSO: Nonstatutory Stock Option
SAR: Stock Appreciation Right
Restricted: Restricted Stock

Source: ECRInfo Database of 1,000 Companies

option is not truly performance-related, because market perceptions determine the value of the award and there is little empirical evidence that corporate performance is improved by granting options. However, the stock option's combination of so many attractive features, both to the Executive and the Company, explains its widespread use as an element of incentive compensation.

The SEC's 1992 rules on disclosure of executive compensation threaten the congenial climate that has surrounded stock options by subjecting them to a triple spotlight. For proxy disclosure purposes, the rules require that (1) options must be valued when they are granted, (2) while options are outstanding, the spread between the grant price and the market price of the stock at the end of the reporting year must be disclosed and (3) when options are exercised, the gain realized by the Executive must be reported.

By thus focusing attention on stock options, the disclosure rules may inhibit their use. Harsh as the spotlight may be, however, both to the Executive and the Company, disclosure should not dictate the design of the compensation package—especially the use of stock options. Their defining qualities, which have led options to be regarded as the almost perfect compensation tool, still apply:

- under current accounting rules (but probably not for much longer), there is no charge to the Company's earnings when an option is granted at 100% of market price,

- the Executive incurs no investment risk before exercise of the option,
- the Executive incurs no tax consequences before exercise of the option,
- the Company does not have to make any cash outlay and, in fact, receives cash when the Executive pays the purchase price upon exercise of the option, and
- the Executive obtains the right to acquire an equity interest in the Company and can share in any long-term growth in the value of the Company's stock.

Most important, stock options ally the Executive with the interest of the shareholders to whom he or she is ultimately responsible and for whose benefit the Company has employed the Executive. Together with dividends, the increase in the value of stock is the measure of a company's performance from the shareholders' point of view.

Shareholders are rarely, if ever, granted options to acquire stock and never on the advantageous terms accorded to executives. These favorable terms cause options to be viewed, rightly, more as compensation than as a pure equity investment opportunity. Nevertheless, options do make executives owners and, thus, help to promote a "family" culture.

Stock options are also frequently offered as an inducement to obtain an Executive's services. When used as a "golden hello," they involve only minimal cost to the Company under current accounting rules.

From an Employer's standpoint, the disadvantage of options is the difficulty of determining grant frequency and the number of options to be granted. While there is no norm for the interval between stock option grants, they are usually made every two or three years, although recently grants have tended to be more frequent.

Nor is there any general rule for an Employer as to the appropriate multiple of the value of option grants to cash compensation (salary plus bonus). In a 1990 survey of 350 companies, the average multiple was 2.4 but the range of multiples extended as high as 115.2.

From the Executive's standpoint, options are a form of compensation that bears minimal risk. Thus, the Executive would like as large a grant as possible, to vest at as early a date as possible.

A classic example is the multiple options granted to Lee A. Iacocca as CEO of Chrysler—often in lieu of salary and bonus—on which the gain, over six years, was $43 million! Another "mega" grant that paid off handsomely was that to Stephen M. Wolf at United Airlines of options to purchase 250,000 shares of UAL stock. The estimated value of these options and his other stock-based compensation in 1990 was $17 million.

In 1991 Leon C. Hirsch, CEO of U.S. Surgical, received options to purchase 2.75 million shares of the company's stock over five years—in recognition of his role as "the architect of a tremendous creation of wealth for the owners of U.S. Surgical." The one million options that he was eligible to exercise in 1992 had a value of approximately $41 million above their grant value of $62 million. The multiple of granted option values to his 1991 cash compensation (approximately $2.5 million) was 45.7 on the one million options and 125.6 on the entire 2.75 million options.

Mega grants of options may need to be more carefully considered in the future, because of their increased visibility under the SEC's 1992 disclosure rules and also because of the likelihood that option grants may have to be charged to earnings.

Options are really a "call" on the assets of the Company. As such, they should not be granted lightly, and their exercisability could be tied to the attainment of preset performance goals within a specified period. With performance-linked vesting, if the goals are not met, the options expire. Alternatively, options could be exercisable only *after* a certain period and then only if the stock reaches a specified price *and* maintains it long enough—say for 20 out of 90 consecutive trading days—to enable shareholders to take advantage of the increased price. Under current accounting practices, such a conditionally exercisable option would probably require a charge to earnings. For this reason conditional grants have not been widely used.

Nevertheless, a few companies have adopted this approach. For example, H. J. Heinz Company granted an option in 1990 to its CEO, Anthony J. O'Reilly, to purchase four million shares of stock. He must exercise these options within one year if the stock reaches a specified price, which is substantially in excess of the exercise price, and holds that price for 10 out of 15 consecutive trading days. ITT granted options in 1991 to more than 500 executives at a price of $51 that are not exercisable until the stock reaches $71.40 and holds that price for 10 consecutive trading days.

Some companies also require that executive optionees retain the stock they acquire through the exercise of options. Among other things, a retention feature prevents a bailout if the executive anticipates a decline in the price of the stock.

An analogous type of option grant that is being increasingly utilized is the premium price option, *i.e.*, an option whose exercise price is above the market price on the date of grant. The 2.5 million options granted to Paul Fireman by Reebok International in 1990 have an average exercise price 18% higher than the price of the company's stock on the date of grant. Recently AT&T adopted a program of premium options for its senior management that makes exercise of three-quarters of the options dependent on increases in the price of the stock ranging from 20% to 50%.

Alternatively—but less acceptably in today's climate—options may be granted at a discount from market price. This affords the Executive an immediate potential profit, but at a cost to the Company, in terms of a charge to earnings equal to the discount.

Quite apart from the success of any effort to develop a universal grant-date valuation formula for stock options, the 1990s may see a change in attitude about the suitability of large grants. At the same time, there is likely to be greater emphasis on techniques that tie the exercisability of options to long-term goals (*e.g.*, performance-linked vesting and premium price options). Also, there may be greater emphasis on techniques that promote share retention, such as stock matching (*i.e.*, matching with additional stock the option shares that an executive holds) and restricted options (*i.e.*, making option shares subject to forfeiture).

Finally, in certain limited situations, transferable options may enable the Executive to achieve significant estate tax savings while benefiting members of his or her family. Transferable options raise complex income and estate tax questions as well as securities law problems. Accordingly, they should be used only after discussion with the Executive's and the Company's legal and tax advisors.

Stock Appreciation Rights ("SARs")

Closely related to stock options are SARs. An SAR is essentially the right to receive the appreciation in value of a share of stock over its value on the date of grant. While SARs have roughly the same economic value to the Executive as stock options, the current accounting treatment is quite different.

Under current accounting rules, SARs—whether payable in stock or cash—require an annual charge to earnings. This requirement has caused many companies to avoid using SARs.

If, as expected, FASB will require an identical charge to earnings for stock options and SARs payable in stock, the use of such SARs is likely to increase, because an Executive can receive the same economic value with a lesser amount of stock.

Under the SEC's 1992 disclosure rules, SARs must be reported in the same detail as indicated above in connection with stock options.

Incentive Shares

Another form of long-term stock compensation involves the award of "incentive shares." While the Executive receives an outright grant of Company stock, the shares are earned only if specified goals, set in advance, are met. Compared with stock options, the potential payout is larger, but there is also a lot more at risk, because the incentive shares may never be earned at all.

Xerox Corporation has adopted such a plan, covering approximately 50 senior executives. The goals are tied to return on assets. Targets are not

reset, so that if one year's target is not met, the next
year's target is all that much higher. Xerox has increased the at-risk factor in its plan by requiring an
executive to purchase one year's salary worth of
Xerox stock as a condition of participation.

Restricted Stock

A third form of long-term stock compensation involves the award of restricted stock—generally the
common stock of the Company issued in connection
with the performance of services and without cost or
for a nominal price. Ownership of the stock is subject to certain conditions or restrictions—such as the
Executive's continued employment for a specified period or the attainment, within a specified period, of
preset goals.

Martin S. Davis, CEO of Gulf & Western,
received in one year an award of 250,000 shares of
restricted stock, valued at $4 million. The following
year he received an additional 100,000 shares. At the
time of the second award, the 250,000 shares had a
value of $12.6 million.

Also, in what is believed to be the largest
stock award ever, Coca-Cola awarded its CEO,
Roberto C. Goizueta, one million shares of restricted
stock—valued at $63.5 million in 1991, the year of
grant (and at $81 million on March 18, 1992)—on
condition that he remain with the company five more

years, until age 65. In justification of what one critic characterized as "more of a gift than an incentive," the company noted that during Mr. Goizueta's 11-year tenure the stock price had risen more than 900%, adding $50 billion to shareholder value.

PERFORMANCE-BASED INCENTIVE PLANS

The other principal type of long-term incentive compensation is performance-based—predicated on the achievement of certain preset goals over a period of time. The award may be paid either in Company stock or cash or both.

Performance-based incentive plans will play an increasingly important role in the 1990s, as companies move to base the compensation of their executives more on the long than the short term and more on performance than salary.

Unless the Executive is to be merely a caretaker, the board of directors must give him or her adequate scope and tether to achieve the mutually agreed objectives. It is this power to make something happen on one's own initiative and in one's own way that is a prime motivating force. If the anticipated results are forthcoming, money should and will reward them. If not, the Executive should be gone—or the compensation renegotiated in the light of changed circumstances.

Appropriate questions about an Executive's incentive opportunity include:

- How large should it be?
- How should it vest and over what period of time?
- How should performance be measured?
- Can intermediate milestones be identified? If so, should their achievement be rewarded?
- If the objectives are achieved in part, but not in whole, should there be a proportionate reward?
- If the objectives are exceeded, should the reward be increased or should it be capped?
- What is fair both to the Company and the Executive?

These are but a few of the questions that must be answered in order to design the "right" performance-based long-term incentive plan. There are no general answers, and it is not within the purview of this book to examine the considerations in depth—only to stress the role of an incentive plan in the Executive's employment arrangements and to indicate some of the factors that will shape its design.

The key to the design of a successful plan is individual tailoring to a specific situation—based on the compensation consultant's expertise, experience and intimate knowledge both of the Company and its strategic objectives and of the Executive and his or her personal agenda. Design is not an exact science but an art. Nevertheless, to serve the Company's purpose of emphasizing long-term performance, the plan must be formula-driven and it must preclude discretionary payout when goals are not met.

The critical issue in the design of most long-term incentive plans is the selection of the proper measure of performance to define the formula. This is always a difficult challenge to management and the board of directors. Not only are there many possible measures—such as increase in net earnings per share, return on equity, return on investment, market share and share price—but appropriate measures vary from industry to industry. Here again, the measure of performance must fit the specific situation.

There are only two useful generalizations:
- The measure must be a valid index of enhancement of shareholder wealth, and
- the Executive must bear the risk of failure to meet the agreed performance objectives.

Triangle Industries affords a good illustration of a performance-based plan. Following a leveraged buyout of National Can Corporation, Triangle adopted a plan that awarded performance incentive units, which would increase or decrease in value over their six-year term based on the earnings per share of Triangle's common stock. The 100,000 units awarded to Nelson Peltz and Peter May, chairman and president respectively, reached their maximum value under the plan in two years, whereupon Peltz and May together received $9 million.

Comments

Employers should strongly favor goal-based long-term incentives as a means to compensate. An Executive's willingness to accept such incentives as the preponderant part of the compensation package is an important indicator of self-confidence—the confidence that his or her performance will produce value and that he or she will have considerable say in determining the measure of performance.

Attitude toward the job may well determine the Executive's perspective on long-term incentives. The Executive who is self-confident or an "entrepreneur" will have no hesitation in accepting a compensation package in which a large part of the value depends on performance. Such an Executive may insist on receiving mega grants of stock options (*viz.* Lee Iacocca and Stephen Wolf, as noted above) or on participating in a tailor-made long-term incentive plan that will pay off handsomely for results.

However, long-term incentive arrangements are not static. An incentive plan developed at the beginning of an employment term is often only a best guess—as to what the Employer expects the Executive to accomplish and is willing to pay for the results and as to what the Executive expects to be able to accomplish and thinks the results are worth.

Companies' situations change, and often quickly. Both Executives and Employers need to monitor results closely and be willing to modify long-term incentive and equity arrangements to meet changed circumstances. The best way to accomplish this is through ongoing involvement of the compensation consultant who designed the arrangements—to track how they "play out" against the agreed performance measures.

TROUBLED COMPANIES

Troubled companies—companies that are in bankruptcy or that run a significant near-term risk of being so—pose a special problem in attracting competent management, which performance-based long-term incentive compensation can be helpful in solving.

This problem is the reluctance of a qualified executive—one who may have the precise talents needed to lead the company out of trouble—to join the crew of a sinking ship. Fear of failure, of future unemployability and of inability to collect the compensation agreed upon combine to make the recruitment of new management particularly difficult.

If the company is in bankruptcy, any arrangements with new management will require the approval of the bankruptcy court. However, such approval will provide the security that the management team is entitled to demand, as well as protection from other creditors should the company fail.

If the company is not in bankruptcy, any arrangements with new management may subsequently prove worthless. While it is possible to secure the payment of future compensation, as discussed below, any effective security technique is likely to give rise to adverse tax consequences to the executive—in the form of current taxation of compensation not yet received, the payment of which has been secured through or guaranteed by a third party.

In order to overcome the understandable hesitancy of an executive to join a troubled company, the reward offered must be commensurate with the additional risk assumed. However, it need not be immediate and in all likelihood cannot be, since more often than not the company will be strapped for cash. Generally, then, the reward for turning around a troubled company will have to be in the form of enhanced equity—either a larger-than-customary number of options to purchase stock or an outright grant of a significant block of stock.

Often, too, a substantial "golden hello" payment will have to be part of the compensation package to induce an executive to join a troubled company.

PRIVATELY HELD COMPANIES

Stock-based plans of privately held companies pose special problems: the method used to measure the value of the privately held stock and the availability of a "market" for the Executive to realize the increase in value of any shares or other stock-based award.

The first problem is usually solved by use of formulas or valuation by outside experts, the second by an obligation on the Company to buy back any securities that the Executive receives.

In many cases, however, the owners of privately held concerns are reluctant to give *any* equity interest to other than family members. If nonfamily executives are part of the management team, "phantom" stock can meet the objective of equity participation without sacrificing the ownership interests of the family. Phantom stock is usually described as units that are equivalent to but are not actual stock of the corporation. The advantage is that units can be paid out in cash.

SECURITY OF PAYMENT

Any long-term compensation arrangement inevitably raises questions about security of payment. Increasingly, executives want assurance that the Company will be able to make good on its commitment to pay deferred compensation when payment is to commence and for the full term of the payment period. Techniques for securing payment are discussed in *Chapter 7* under "Supplemental Retirement Benefits."

With regard to deferred bonuses, securing payment may not be appropriate, particularly if the Executive can elect whether or not to defer receipt of a bonus: The Executive who elects to defer may be said to have assumed the risk of nonpayment. However, when the Executive must defer, security of payment is a legitimate concern that needs to be addressed by both the Executive and the Employer.

7

BENEFITS AND
PERQUISITES

THE PURPOSE of employee benefits is to provide financial protection upon the occurrence of certain adverse events: death, disability, retirement and illness or injury.

The difference between benefits provided to Executives and those provided to employees is generally one of magnitude rather than type.

Customarily, Executives receive additional life insurance, as well as supplemental retirement, disability and medical benefits above the levels provided under the Company's tax-qualified and group benefit plans. The question, then, is not the kind of benefits the Executive will receive, but their extent and the manner of providing them (Fig. 4).

Special problems arise when the Executive is posted overseas, especially if he or she is employed by a foreign entity. Then the Executive needs to be certain that the benefits match those that would be received in the United States.

FIGURE 4

SUPPLEMENTAL BENEFITS
AT 1,000 PUBLIC COMPANIES
1991

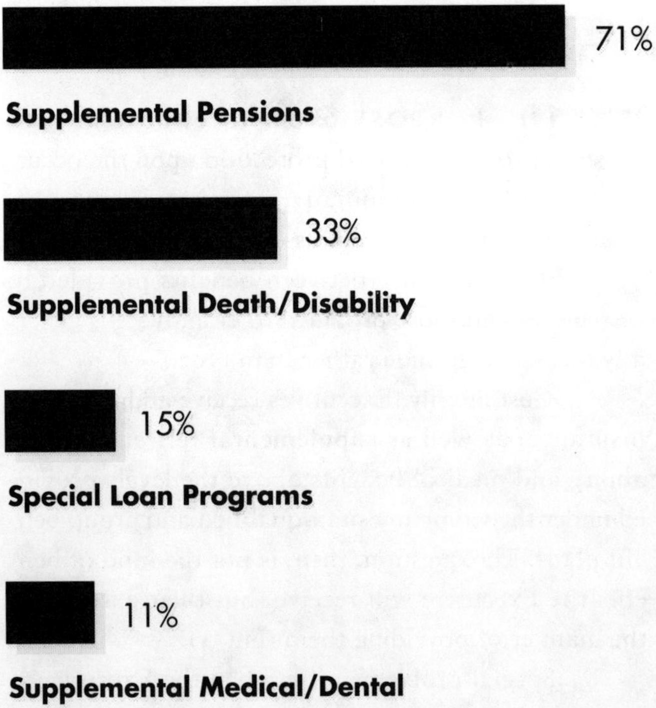

71%

Supplemental Pensions

33%

Supplemental Death/Disability

15%

Special Loan Programs

11%

Supplemental Medical/Dental

Source: ECRInfo Database of 1,000 Companies

BENEFITS

Life Insurance

Group life insurance plans provide generous death benefits to employees, but such benefits are generally capped at a lower level than Executives feel will afford adequate protection for their surviving dependents.

Accordingly, Companies are usually willing to provide additional life insurance protection to the Executive, either in the form of term insurance or whole-life insurance on a shared basis—split-dollar insurance.

Under a split-dollar plan, the Executive pays only the cost of term insurance and the Company pays the cost of whole life insurance. The arrangement constitutes a low-interest premium loan from the Company to the Executive. After a specified period or upon the death of the Executive, the Company recovers its premium payments in full. If recovery occurs before the Executive's death, the policy is thenceforth self-sustaining.

If the Executive's employment terminates before the Company recovers the full amount of its premiums—assuming that the Company is not obligated to make further premium payments—the Executive may buy out the policy and either assume the entire cost of the policy or maintain the policy at a reduced level of coverage or with an extended premium-payment period or both.

Reebok International maintains a $50 million split-dollar plan on the life of its CEO, Paul B. Fireman. The annual premium is approximately $500,000.

Under the SEC's 1992 rules for disclosure of executive compensation, disclosure of split-dollar life insurance coverage is required: The amount of Company-paid premiums must be included in the Executive's reported annual compensation.

As a benchmark for the amount of additional insurance to be provided, the Company should consider insurance equal to a multiple, up to five, of the Executive's salary or cash compensation for the final year during the intended term of employment.

Life insurance is an essential financial planning instrument for most Executives. To serve its purpose in meeting family needs, it should be integrated with the individual's retirement and estate planning. If the need for protection extends beyond the employment term, as it almost always does, certain life insurance arrangements offer attractive and innovative long-term estate planning opportunities on a highly cost-effective basis to both the Executive and the Company.

In a very real sense, the Executive and the Company are partners in the Executive's financial and estate plan. This is particularly true when corporate-sponsored life insurance is used; if properly structured, it can provide substantial family benefits, often at low or no cost to the Executive. At the same time, the corporate sponsor can recoup its premium payments over time.

Recent developments include programs that provide insurance on the lives of the Executive and his or her spouse for the benefit of family members; this form of "survivorship" insurance pays benefits upon the death of the second to die. Such a program is an effective planning technique when combined with and viewed as part of a broad family-based financial plan, and it costs substantially less than single-life coverage on the Executive alone.

Disability Benefits

Executives are usually not adequately protected under regular long-term disability plans against the risk of loss of income due to permanent disability. Ideally, disability benefits should replace approximately 60%-65% of salary, at least up to a certain level; above that level the percentage should decrease or the dollar amount should be capped. The Executive should ascertain the level of disability benefits provided by the Company and, if necessary, seek to obtain supplemental benefits.

Medical Benefits

The Executive will also have serious concerns about the medical plans in which he or she is to participate. Sometimes the Executive will be allowed 100% reimbursement for medical expenses rather than the customary 80%, on the basis that the Company wants to eliminate worries over medical costs that could keep the individual from concentrating fully on its affairs.

In some cases the Executive may ask for lifetime medical coverage. Whether or not the Company should provide such coverage depends on a number of factors, such as:

- the existence of special medical needs among the Executive's dependents,
- the extent of the medical benefits provided by the Executive's previous employer, and
- the perceived value of the Executive to the Company.

Supplemental Life, Medical and Disability Benefits

Life insurance, medical insurance and long-term disability insurance are fairly standard arrangements, and supplemental insurance is almost always available to cover part, if not all, of these risks.

If possible, medical benefits should be provided through insurance, because under current law benefits received pursuant to an uninsured plan must be included in the Executive's taxable income.

It may not be possible to obtain insured disability benefits up to the desired level from a domestic carrier. In this event, the Company may choose to self-insure the supplemental coverage or seek to obtain the desired level of individual coverage from a foreign carrier.

The Company can also consider raising the disability benefits under its group plan, but such a move is not without cost. If insured supplemental disability benefits can be obtained, the Executive should pay the premiums. Then, under current law, any benefits received will be tax-free. When the Company pays the premiums, benefits are taxable to the Executive.

When supplemental "welfare" benefits are provided through individual insurance contracts—which is generally the case with life insurance and disability benefits—the benefits are "portable." This means that they can follow the Executive whose employment terminates prior to retirement if he or she is willing to assume the cost of continued coverage. In this situation, portability may represent a substantial economic benefit because of the typically high levels of supplemental coverage. Indeed, it may relieve the individual who does not anticipate having subsequent group coverage of the need to replace the corresponding benefits.

Unlike supplemental life insurance and disability benefits, supplemental medical benefits are not generally provided under *individual* insurance contracts and, thus, are not generally portable. Absent portability, the Executive whose employment terminates must rely on the legally mandated post-termi-

nation coverage applicable to group medical plans—
"COBRA"—or on the conversion features applicable
to the Company's plans.

The Executive should consider negotiating
portability of supplemental welfare benefits as part
of the employment arrangements. Commencement of
employment, when he or she has the most leverage,
is the time to do so.

Supplemental Retirement Benefits

The Executive may also need to replace "lost" retirement benefits from a previous employer. Usually benefits are lost when the Executive's prior service was
too brief, or earnings too low, to permit accrual and
vesting of meaningful retirement benefits. Executives
are especially vulnerable to this risk, because of limits
on the amount of benefits that they can receive from
tax-qualified plans and because of their mobility. Accordingly, the greater part of their retirement benefits usually comes from a nonqualified plan, under
which vesting is often deferred until retirement. Thus
an Executive whose prior employment terminated before retirement may lose significant benefits.

Supplemental retirement arrangements tend
to be costly, particularly for an older Executive who
will have a relatively short employment period (less
than 10 years) with the Company. Executives should
be sensitive to these costs, which can run to several

hundred thousands of dollars per year, a cost that is a charge against the Company's earnings. In the case of one individual who was being considered for CEO of the North American operations of a major European bank, the negotiations ultimately foundered on the Executive's insistence upon expensive supplemental retirement arrangements.

The Executive, particularly if transferring in mid-career from one employer to another, usually wishes assurance that retirement benefits will be equal to or greater than those in the prior position. From the Executive's standpoint, accrual and vesting of any supplemental retirement benefits should take place over the shortest possible time. From the Company's standpoint, vesting should be deferred—for as long as five years and possibly until retirement. In this way, supplemental retirement benefits can serve as "golden handcuffs" for the Executive whom the Company wishes to retain. Regardless of the number of years of employment, the Executive should not have any rights at all if he or she is terminated for cause.

The Company should quite rightly view supplemental benefits as part of the Executive's total compensation package. If their cost is substantial, it may affect how much the Company is willing to offer in other parts of the package, *e.g.*, salary or bonus.

The Executive is concerned not only with the design and amount of supplemental retirement benefits but also with securing their payment. At the same time, the Executive does not wish to pay taxes currently for retirement income to be received in the future. Balancing of these two objectives—security for the payment of benefits and protection against adverse income tax consequences—is the principal challenge in providing this type of benefit.

A number of techniques are available, among them:

- a grantor ("rabbi") trust,
- Company-owned life insurance,
- a "secular" trust,
- purchase by the Company and transfer to the Executive of one or more annuity contracts, and
- purchase by the Company of a surety contract that guarantees payment if the Company does not make good on its obligation.

Each of these and other available techniques has its advantages and disadvantages.

A rabbi trust is a trust for the benefit of the Executive the assets of which, however, are subject to the creditors of the Company in the event of its insolvency or bankruptcy. This condition causes the assets of the trust to be viewed as part of the general assets of the Company. As a result, there is no immediate taxation when assets are transferred to the trust, but the trust affords only limited security to the Executive.

Company-owned life insurance affords even less security for the Executive because, in addition to being an asset of the Company subject to the claims of creditors, it is subject to the Company's control.

A secular trust, which is not subject to creditors' rights and the assets of which are separate from those of the Company, affords the most security to the Executive but, at the same time, is a costly way of securing benefits. This is because the Company must forever relinquish control over the trust assets and—to shield the Executive from adverse tax consequences and make the arrangement palatable—it may have to "gross up" the Executive for the tax on the income from the trust assets. Such a trust was established in 1988 for James Wood, chairman of A&P, and funded with an initial contribution of over $10 million!

The purchase of and transfer to the Executive of one or more annuity contracts also affords ultimate security to the Executive but again, for the same reasons, this may involve tax gross-ups at a cost that makes this alternative unacceptable to the Company.

Similarly, surety arrangements utilizing third-party insurers may entail immediate adverse tax consequences to the Executive.

The Executive should seek to maximize the security of future retirement benefits even at the expense of immediate unfavorable tax consequences. A secular trust or Executive-owned annuity policies will best achieve this result.

Generally speaking, Companies are sensitive to the Executive's needs and are willing to provide a supplemental layer of protection. Supplemental benefits can be costly and, if provided through individually tailored arrangements, as is usually the case, they can have a significant effect on the earnings of the Company. Also, supplemental benefits provided to the CEO and the four highest-paid executives of a publicly traded company must be disclosed in the annual proxy statement.

"Costly" is a relative term, however, and the Company should weigh the cost of providing supplemental benefits against the perceived value of the Executive. The cost of supplemental benefits is only one component of the Executive's compensation package and, in most cases, not a major component, especially if the Executive's employment continues for many years.

The Company will usually resist providing *secured* nonqualified retirement benefits, because of their cost and the loss of control over the assets dedicated to them. If the Company is willing to secure the benefits, this is all the more reason to impose stringent vesting requirements on the Executive's right to receive them.

PERQUISITES

Perquisites are a fixture of compensation, particularly for high-level executives. While they are not costly relative to other compensation as a whole, they have high visibility and, as a consequence, can cause resentment among rank-and-file employees and even, on occasion, draw the ire of shareholders. For these reasons, it is in the interest of both the Company and the

Executive to keep perquisites in the right perspective.

Perquisites are less commonly extended than they used to be. Their visibility has caused them to become a prime target for corporate cost cutting. Also, with lower income tax rates on cash compensation, perquisites have become less attractive to Executives and there has been less reason to pay compensation in this form. Moreover, some perquisites are taxable to the Executive to the extent that they are used for personal purposes.

While perquisites may not be cut back or discontinued for incumbent Executives, the individual moving to a new position as CEO may find that fewer perquisites are offered. In this instance, the Executive may be able to negotiate, as part of a sign-on bonus, an amount to compensate for the perquisites that he or she is losing. This will require a careful analysis of their monetary value—as distinguished in some instances from their prestige value.

So long as the type and level of perquisites extended by the Company are reasonable and bear a reasonable relationship to the performance of the Executive's duties, there should be little ground for objection. For example, it is in the Company's interest that the Executive receive competent tax and financial advice. Not only does this particular perquisite relieve the Executive of anxiety and enable him or her to perform more effectively, but it also leaves the Executive less open to the exposure and bad publicity that can arise from filing incorrect or even fraudulent tax returns. Similarly, it is in both the Company's and the Executive's interest that the Executive be healthy, and annual physical examinations can help to meet this objective.

The biggest problems are the abuse of perquisites by the Executive and the continuation of perquisites after termination of employment. Abuse is self-explanatory, but the continuation of perquisites following the Executive's termination is less often addressed. The Executive wishes perquisites to continue for as long as possible. From the Company's point of view, however, continuation of perquisites after termination is seldom desirable because of their high visibility.

An exception to this general rule is the provision of tax and financial advice for at least one year following the Executive's termination of employment. As termination is often unexpected and not of the Executive's own choosing, it is a time when the Executive may be most in need of this perquisite.

Regular Perquisites

Typical perquisites include:
- a car and driver,
- membership in a country club and possibly also a luncheon club,
- an annual physical examination, and
- tax and financial counseling.

Less typical perquisites include:
- housing,

- a security system for the Executive's residence, and
- a corporate airplane.

Special Perquisites for Overseas Service

Overseas service often involves special perquisites not ordinarily provided in the United States, because of the added expense of relocation and foreign residence and the frequent need for tighter personal security. Examples are:

- airfare to and from the United States at least once a year for the Executive and immediate family members,
- a furnished residence,
- a car and specially trained security driver,
- tuition aid for children,
- tax equalization, and
- a cost-of-living differential.

CHAPTER

8

TERMINATION OF EMPLOYMENT AND CONSEQUENCES OF TERMINATION

A N EMPLOYMENT AGREEMENT serves two basic purposes: It sets forth the duties and obligations of the Company and the Executive while the Executive is employed, and the rights and obligations of each following termination of the Executive's employment.

As often as not, it is the second purpose that is of primary concern to the Executive. So long as things go smoothly, *i.e.*, while employment continues, the Executive has little concern with the consequences of termination. However, when termination occurs, particularly if it is not at the initiative of the Executive, the picture changes radically. For this reason alone, the rights and obligations of the respective parties should be clearly and fully set forth. Also, properly conceived termination provisions can preclude expensive and time-consuming litigation.

TERMINATION DUE TO DEATH

If an Executive's employment terminates due to death, the consequences are fairly straightforward.

The primary benefit that accrues to the survivors is, of course, the insurance carried on the Executive's life. For a high-level executive, this is usually substantial and it obviates the need for any significant salary continuation.

Customarily, salary is paid through the date of death, but the employment agreement may provide that it will be paid for a specified period thereafter (such as six months or a year).

A bonus for the year in which death occurs may be paid on a *pro rata* basis, with the amount dependent upon the performance of the Company determined at the end of the year.

Payments from long-term arrangements, such as stock options and incentive compensation, are usually governed by the terms of the particular plan.

Employment agreements frequently provide that medical benefits will be continued for the Executive's survivors, if not for life, at least for a period of years. In view of increasing medical costs and the frequent difficulty of obtaining appropriate insurance, continuation of medical benefits should be a prime concern to the Executive even if the survivors must shoulder all or part of the cost.

Most advantageous from the Executive's standpoint is continuation of medical coverage under the

Company's regular insured or self-insured medical plan. It is less costly both to the Company and the Executive's survivors (if they must pay for continued coverage): Group rates apply, and a group plan is less likely to be terminated or changed. However, if survivors cannot be covered under the Company's plan, the Executive should seek to have the Company provide post-death survivor medical benefits on an individual basis.

TERMINATION DUE TO DISABILITY

Termination of the Executive's employment due to disability raises two issues: the definition of disability and the level of disability benefits.

Definition of Disability

The Executive generally wishes to avoid termination due to "disability" as defined in the Company's group disability plan. To accomplish this, the employment agreement should use a special definition of disability—such as the Executive's inability to perform duties under the employment agreement for reasons of mental or physical disability for a period of 180 consecutive days or for more than 270 days in any 365-day period.

As an additional protection, the employment agreement may provide that the determination of disability will be made by a physician of the Company's choice, so long as the Executive agrees to the determination. If the Executive does not agree, the Company and the Executive may each choose a physician who, if they do not agree, will select a third physician to make such determination.

Level of Disability Benefits

More important is the level of disability benefits to be paid. Because benefits under a group disability plan are usually insufficient to provide adequate replacement income, the Executive should seek to have supplemental disability benefits. A typical amount of replacement income is 60%-65% of the Executive's salary up to a certain amount and above that level a lesser percentage. In some cases, disability benefits are based on total cash compensation (including any annual bonus), but employers and insurers are usually reluctant to adopt this larger base.

Employment agreements also often provide for salary continuation for a specified period after termination due to disability, such as six months or a year. When they do, salary is reduced by the amount of disability benefits that the Executive receives.

Disability benefits are usually paid until the date when the Executive would normally have retired, *e.g.*, age 62 or age 65, unless the disability terminates earlier and the Executive returns to work.

Employee Benefits During Disability

Critically important to the Executive is the continuation of employee benefits during disability. If this is not the Company's normal practice, the Executive should seek to have the employment agreement provide that medical and life insurance coverage and the accrual of retirement benefits will continue during the period of disability.

Other benefits payable to the Executive upon termination of employment are usually determined by the practices of the Company or the terms of particular plans. Such benefits include the exercise of stock options and, sometimes, the acceleration of payment of long-term compensation awards.

TERMINATION FOR CAUSE

Because the consequences of termination for "cause" are so drastic—usually the immediate cessation of all payments to the Executive—negotiations over this provision are often lengthy and difficult. Critical is the definition of cause; without a controlling definition, cause will be interpreted under applicable state law. The usual open-ended provisions of state law are more favorable to employers than employees.

The Executive naturally wants to have as narrow a definition of cause as possible. Conversely, the Employer prefers a wider definition, giving it more latitude to terminate an unsatisfactory Executive with minimal expense.

The following definition of cause is highly favorable to the Executive:

(1) the conviction of the Executive of a felony or

(2) the Executive's willful gross misconduct or willful gross neglect of his or her duties which, in either case, has resulted in material economic harm to the Company unless the Executive, in good faith, believed that his or her actions were in the best interests of the Company.

Many Companies will be reluctant to accept this definition of cause. A broader definition would include such reasons as disobedience to directions of the board of directors, drug or alcohol abuse or conduct involving fraud or dishonesty.

Sometimes the definition of cause specifies the Executive's *indictment* for a felony, rather than conviction. Obviously this definition is more favorable to the Company.

Whatever the definition, the Executive should insist on the opportunity, prior to discharge, to defend the actions giving rise to termination for cause before an appropriate tribunal of the Company. The tribunal is usually the board of directors, and the Executive is given the right to appear before the board with counsel. Also, "due process" provisions often permit the Executive to correct the actions complained of, except for conviction of a felony.

Care is needed to see that the definition of cause is limited to actions that adversely affect the Company. Cause can include actions that affect the *reputation* of the Company, such as unbecoming public conduct, as well as actions that have a more immediate economic impact.

Employers should give careful thought to an expanded definition of cause that embraces termination for failure of the Executive to meet agreed performance goals. Safeguards can be built in to protect the Executive against unsatisfactory performance due to factors beyond his or her control.

The usual consequence of termination for cause is cutoff of all payments to the Executive as of that date—except for any awards made prior to termination but not yet paid. The Employer should have the right to impose the additional consequence of forfeiture of all of the Executive's accrued supplemental retirement benefits.

TERMINATION WITHOUT CAUSE

At the heart of the termination provisions of an executive employment agreement is termination without cause, because it is the situation in which the Executive's post-termination compensation and benefits will be greatest.

On its face, termination without cause means

just what it says, but usually it also includes "constructive" termination, *i.e.,* the occurrence of certain events that are treated as if the Employer had terminated the Executive's employment without cause. Constructive termination is often more important, and occurs more frequently, than actual termination without cause. Accordingly, the definition of constructive termination is critical.

Constructive Termination

Among the circumstances usually constituting constructive termination without cause are the following:

- loss of position or titles, including board membership if applicable,
- assignment of duties or responsibilities inconsistent with the position or positions for which the Executive has been employed,
- decrease in salary or bonus opportunity,
- change in location of the Executive's employment, or
- decrease in the benefits to which the Executive is entitled, *unless* such decrease is part of an across-the-board decrease affecting all high-level executives of the Company.

A less frequent circumstance of constructive termination is unreasonable interference, in the good-faith judgment of the Executive, in the performance of his or her duties by the Employer or by a major shareholder.

Employers should try to limit the events that can give rise to constructive termination. Generally, change in employment location should not be included, because this is usually within the Executive's control. More to the point, employment location does not affect the Executive's overall responsibilities to the Employer.

Similarly, Employers need to consider whether justified salary decreases should give rise to constructive termination. Further, a distinction should be drawn between a decrease in bonus *opportunity* and a decrease in the amount of the bonus itself.

Consequences of Termination Without Cause

Even as the consequences of termination for cause are drastic for the Executive, so are the consequences of termination without cause drastic for the Company: Generally, the Company is obligated to pay substantial sums to the Executive.

Most employment agreements provide that in the event of termination without cause the Executive is entitled, until the end of the term of the agreement, to the continuation of:

- salary,

- annual bonuses, based on a measure such as the average of previous annual bonuses or the highest previous annual bonus, and
- participation in employee benefit plans, including accrual of pension benefits under any nonqualified arrangement.

Generally also, the employment agreement will provide for acceleration of the exercisability of options (unless the particular stock option plan itself so provides).

Benefits less often included in the event of termination without cause are:

- continued participation in life insurance and disability plans and
- continuation of any perquisites to which the Executive was entitled.

If the term of employment is for a long period—four or more years—the Employer may not want to continue payments until the end of the term. Conversely, an Executive nearing the end of the term will favor post-termination payments that extend beyond the term of employment. One way to avoid the protracted payments that may arise from early termination—and to protect the Executive from the consequences of late-in-term termination—is to provide post-termination payments for the remainder of the term subject both to a minimum and maximum time limit.

Continuation of Benefits

Employment agreements usually provide that benefits such as life insurance and medical insurance will continue until the end of the term of the agreement or until the Executive obtains equivalent coverage from another employer.

Legal prohibitions may prevent the Employer from continuing some benefits. Such prohibitions usually relate to tax-qualified pension and profit-sharing plans. To guard against the loss of particular benefits, employment agreements often provide that if a particular benefit may not be legally continued, the Executive is entitled to receive its "economic equivalent."

Economic equivalent is usually defined in terms of the insurance premium that the Executive would have to pay on an individual basis to obtain the benefit. Less often, it is defined by the amount of the lost benefit itself.

Obligation to Seek Subsequent Employment/Set-Off

Termination-without-cause provisions generally cover the obligation to seek subsequent employment, sometimes requiring the Executive to do so, other times not. In either case, from the Executive's viewpoint, the employment agreement should provide that any amounts received from a subsequent employer will not offset the amounts due from the Employer following termination without cause.

Employers may view such a provision as a disincentive to the Executive to seek subsequent employment and, for that reason, they often insist on at least a partial offset.

Constructive termination-without-cause provisions also generally permit the Company to rectify or cure the triggering incident within a specified period of time. Because of the drastic consequences for the Company, in terms of the substantial amounts that may be due the Executive, this is not unreasonable.

Termination Following a Change in Control

Special considerations apply in the case of termination without cause following a "change in control" of the Company:

- definition of change in control,
- determination of the compensation and benefits to which the Executive is entitled,
- securing payment of the amounts to which the Executive is entitled, and
- dealing with the possible adverse tax consequences, for the Executive and the Company, of any payments to be made.

The difficult questions relating to the definition of change in control are not a subject of this book. Suffice it to say that any definition is usually couched in terms of change in ownership of a specified percentage of the Company's stock or change in composition of the board of directors from the board that was in place when the Executive was hired. The definition in the Executive's employment agreement should be the same as that used by the Company for other purposes, such as stock option and other long-term incentive plans. Consistency will benefit both the Executive and the Company.

Often, stock options and other incentive awards become automatically exercisable or payable upon a change in control. The Employer needs to weigh the desirability of this feature and consider making certain types of deferred compensation payable only if the change in control benefits the shareholders, as determined by an independent expert. This limitation should not apply to a change in control opposed by management.

The Executive has a legitimate interest in securing payment of the compensation and benefits to which he or she may be entitled upon termination without cause following a change in control. The Employer should be willing to accommodate this interest by providing for payment in a lump sum. However, upon a change in control, the requirement of lump-sum payment may present liquidity problems for the acquiring entity.

Payments to the Executive following a change in control that equal or exceed three times his or her average compensation for the preceding five years ("base compensation") will trigger adverse tax consequences—both for the Executive and the Company. The effect of this limitation may be to deprive the Executive of substantial amounts of compensation and benefits otherwise due.

Accordingly, the Company may agree to make change-in-control payments to the Executive without reference to the limitation imposed by the Internal Revenue Code and let each suffer the resulting tax consequences: for the Executive, a 20% excise tax in addition to the normal income tax liability, and for the Company, loss of a deduction for any amount paid to the Executive in excess of base compensation when the payment equals or exceeds the "three-times" limitation.

A more costly alternative is to make payments without reference to the limitation *and* provide that the Company will gross up the Executive for the tax on the amounts received. The rationale for this approach is that the Executive should not be penalized by taxes that would not have been imposed had not the change in control and termination occurred (Fig. 5).

Because this alternative can be extremely expensive—witness the payment of $29.4 million to F. Ross Johnson after the buy-out of RJR Nabisco—Employers should consider carefully whether they wish to adopt it, even though the gross-up payments

FIGURE 5

TOP EXECUTIVE GOLDEN
PARACHUTE AGREEMENTS

(IN EFFECT IN 1991)

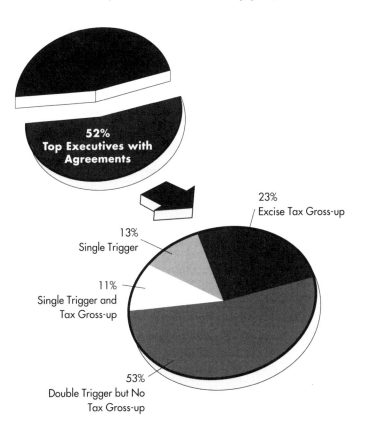

**52%
Top Executives with
Agreements**

23%
Excise Tax Gross-up

13%
Single Trigger

11%
Single Trigger and
Tax Gross-up

53%
Double Trigger but No
Tax Gross-up

Single Trigger: Severance is payable automatically, or
upon voluntary termination, following a change in control.
Double Trigger: Severance is payable upon involuntary
termination following a change in control.

Source: ECRInfo Database of 1,000 Companies

will be made by a successor in interest. They should also determine if this course is really in the best interest of the Company and its shareholders, especially in the climate of the 1990s.

The popularity of "golden parachutes" appears to have peaked, with their place likely to be taken by more modest severance arrangements. At the same time, change-in-control payments—those at as well as above the statutory limit—are coming under increasing scrutiny by shareholders. Indeed, the SEC has already ruled that proxy resolutions may properly subject golden parachute payments to shareholder approval. Just the prospect of such a vote was enough to persuade Consolidated Freightways to cancel termination payments of $7.4 million for eight senior officers.

In troubled businesses, change-in-control payments are under challenge not only by shareholders but also by creditors and regulatory authorities.

VOLUNTARY TERMINATION

Few Employers would attempt to retain the services of the Executive who wishes to leave. On the other hand, the Executive needs protection from the possibility that the Company may seek to obtain damages for breach of contract because of termination prior to the end of the employment term.

For this reason, employment arrangements usually provide that the Executive may voluntarily terminate employment subject to being bound by an agreement not to disclose confidential information. In a voluntary termination, the Executive is usually not entitled to further compensation or benefits.

EARLY TERMINATION

Tenure among CEOs has been declining over the past decade. In the last two years alone, two dozen CEOs left their companies or were ousted after a year or less in the position (Fig. 6). Whereas newcomers used to have a year or more to prove themselves, the "grace period" is now about six months.

When Robert C. Stempel resigned as chairman and CEO after 27 months in 1992, the board of directors of General Motors made clear that his successor as CEO, John F. Smith, Jr., would not enjoy even that limited tenure without success in reversing the company's large losses of the last several years.

Despite short-term pressures, especially in a recessionary environment, early terminations are not always for cause; sometimes they are voluntary—as when a CEO who was brought in to turn a company around effects a merger and is left without enough to do. Sometimes, also, a mismatch occurs when a CEO moves from one industry to another.

When a CEO has been lured with a large

"golden hello," it is not uncommon now for the company to require repayment if the individual terminates voluntarily within a specified period. Thus, when Glen H. Hiner became chairman and CEO of Owens-Corning Fiberglas in 1992 at age 58, he received a $900,000 sign-on bonus and the company agreed to replace his pension from General Electric, where he had been a senior executive. In return, he agreed to pay "liquidated damages" of $1,350,000 if he left within a year "without good reason." The amount reduces to $225,000 after three years on the job.

PUBLIC ANNOUNCEMENT OF EXECUTIVE'S TERMINATION

Termination of the Executive's employment by retirement, death or disability does not pose public relations problems for either the Company or the Executive. Any other termination, particularly for cause or—more often—for unsatisfactory performance, can give rise to problems.

If employment terminates for negative reasons, the Executive has an interest in reducing the adverse "fallout" by seeking to exert some control over any public announcement. Ideally, he or she would like veto power over all publicity, including intra-Company releases. Few companies will or should grant such broad authority, and it is unreasonable for an Executive to expect to have complete control. The

FIGURE 6

1992-1993 EARLY EXECUTIVE TERMINATIONS

TENURE	COMPANY	EXECUTIVE	TERMINATION
36 Months	Shoney's Inc.	Leonard H. Roberts Chairman and CEO	Dec. 1992
31 Months	Ames Dept. Stores	Stephen L. Pistner Chairman and CEO	Dec. 1992
30 Months	Westinghouse Electric Corp.	Paul E. Lego Chairman and CEO	Jan. 1993
27 Months	General Motors	Robert C. Stempel Chairman and CEO	Oct. 1992
18 Months	Chiron Corp.	Hollings C. Renton President and COO	July 1993
18 Months	Rubbermaid	Walter C. Williams Chairman and CEO	Nov. 1992
13 Months	National Data Corp.	O. G. Greene President and CEO	May 1992
11 Months	Glacier Water Services Inc.	Jerry Welch Chariman and CEO	Sept. 1992
11 Months	TransTechnology Corp.	Michael J. Berthelot V. Chmn., Pres., CEO	Aug. 1992
9 Months	JWO Inc.	David L. Sokol President and COO	Oct. 1992
9 Months	Cyprus Minerals Co.	Chester B. Stone, Jr. President and CEO	Feb. 1992
9 Months	Seagram Co.	William G. Pietersen Pres., Tropicana Unit	Oct. 1992
6 Months	BankAmerica Corp.	Robert H. Smith President and COO	Oct. 1992

Executive should be content with a voice in any proposed public announcement.

Employers quite naturally wish to put as good a face as possible on an undesirable termination. Often an announcement that the Executive terminated employment "to pursue other interests" will suffice. Other times something more is needed, in which case the Company should initiate "damage control" procedures as quickly as possible.

Finally, if appropriate, the separation agreement itself may prohibit both the Company and the Executive from making any comment or statement concerning the terms and conditions of the Executive's termination of employment.

CHAPTER

9

RESTRICTIONS ON COMPETITION

⌒

NONCOMPETITION CLAUSES are almost universal in high-level executive employment agreements. From the Executive's point of view, such provisions should specify the organizations with which the Executive may not accept employment. The Employer prefers a description of competing organizations rather than a specific list, as a descriptive provision is more likely to have wider application.

While noncompetition covenants are not easily drafted—because they include complex definitions of time, geographic limitations and descriptions of competitive activity—they are, nonetheless, more easily drafted than enforced. There is a judicial bias against such covenants, with courts tending to find them overbroad, unreasonably burdensome or unnecessary for a company's protection. In some states they are statutorily prohibited and in others they are enforceable only when trade secrets are involved.

This being so, the Employer may wish to include a provision in the employment agreement that the Executive is obligated to inform his or her new employer of the existence of noncompetition restrictions and, if he or she does not do so, the Company has the right to make such disclosure. While disclosure of this sort will not prevent the Executive from going to a competitor, it will put the competitor on notice and, thus, in a disadvantageous position should the Company attempt to enforce the noncompetition provision by court action.

Noncompetition provisions also usually contain sanctions, the most common being cutoff of any post-termination benefits if the Executive accepts employment with a competitor. The Executive may desire a provision that affords a choice between being allowed to compete at the price of foregoing post-termination benefits and abiding by the noncompetition restrictions and receiving such benefits.

Many Employers may be reluctant to permit such a choice, although to do so is consistent with public policy and with the realities of the marketplace. If the Company is really serious about noncompetition, it can make post-termination benefits subject to forfeiture if the Executive competes during a specified period. The more the Executive has to lose, the less likely it is that he or she will compete.

NONDISCLOSURE OF
CONFIDENTIAL
INFORMATION

W HILE COMPANIES are protected
against their employees' unauthorized
disclosure of "confidential information"
by common law and often by statute, the types of
confidential information protected are limited—generally to proprietary information such as customer
lists and trade secrets.

The Employer usually wants to expand the
definition of confidential information to include
such matters as financial information, marketing
plans and product development strategies. An expanded definition of confidential information along
these lines is a legitimate concern of the Company,
and no responsible Executive should object to such a
definition.

On the other hand, the Executive should be
protected when disclosure of confidential information
is required either by a court order or by governmental
authorities having regulatory or supervisory respon-

sibilities over the Company or pursuant to a subpoena of a legislative body or one of its committees.

If nondisclosure of confidential information is not the subject of a separate agreement, it should be covered in the employment agreement itself, and appropriate sanctions provided for its enforcement. Such sanctions usually include cutoff of any post-termination benefits and permission to the Company to seek injunctive relief.

AUTHORITIES

⤳

IN ONE INSTANCE—the authority to negotiate and execute an employment agreement and to adopt ancillary arrangements—the interests of the Executive and the Employer tend to converge.

It goes without saying that the Executive has the authority to bind himself or herself. The Company is different: The nature of high-level employment arrangements is sufficiently exceptional that normally no one individual has the authority to bind it. Thus the Company should obtain the approval of the compensation committee of the board of directors and of the board itself.

As the moving party, so to speak, the compensation committee must have the comfort level necessary to endorse the arrangements as its own. Then it must recommend and justify them to the board. The board, in turn, must satisfy itself that the arrangements are fair and reasonable and in the best interest of the Company's shareholders.

In today's climate, it is to the advantage of both the Executive and the Company to obtain as broad a consensus as possible in support of proposed employment arrangements. Adding emphasis to this point are the 1992 SEC rules on proxy statement disclosure, which submit executive compensation to far greater scrutiny by shareholders than previously.

Accordingly, and despite the practical difficulties, the Employer should consider making high-level employment arrangements subject to ratification, if not approval, by shareholders. While the Executive may be reluctant to take such a risk, approval will go a long way to protect the Company from attack by shareholders. The Executive, of course, will obtain similar protection. The shareholders of Toys "R" Us were asked to, and in 1984 did, give specific approval to Charles Lazarus's compensation arrangements.

Also, it is almost universal practice, because of various legal requirements, that shareholders approve stock option plans and other stock-based incentive plans.

The Employer should obtain from the Executive a covenant that he or she is under no restriction or impediment in accepting employment with the Company.

CONCLUSION

T HE PROMOTION of a senior executive to a new level of responsibility is a watershed event—for the individual especially but also for the employing entity.

For the individual, it must be a call to action, because the consequences of change are too many, too profound and too enduring to be ignored or left to others to dictate. It is a time for the individual to take stock, plan the future and decide where he or she wants to be at the end of the road—and then determine, with professional assistance, how the future employment and compensation arrangements can help to advance the personal agenda. It is also the critical moment for a thorough review of the individual's long-term financial plan and estate plan. Employment arrangements, retirement benefits and estate plan are a continuum and must be treated as such. To succeed, the several elements need to be coordinated one with another.

For the employing entity, this is the time to establish or update its purposes and priorities and institutionalize them through the employment and compensation arrangements. The employer must determine what it wants from the executive, how to get it and how much to pay for it and in what form. This too will require professional assistance.

The objective is an informed and careful matching of the executive's needs and expectations with the company's needs, expectations and financial constraints, so that the executive will be challenged to perform and freed from major financial worries. At the same time the company must be assured, to the extent possible, that its strategic goals are understood and endorsed and will be energetically advanced.

A meeting of minds, a coming together from two directions, marks the end of the process—but only the beginning of what should be a long-term relationship. Like all good relationships, however, the one between executive and employer will require continued effort on both sides and mutual supportiveness. Often too, it will require professional assistance.

To aid both senior executives and their current or future employers, we include on the following pages a list of points to consider as they start the process of designing, negotiating and implementing successful employment and compensation arrangements.

Good fortune to both parties!

Checklist of Points to Consider

Discussion Points for Employment and Compensation Arrangements Between ABC Company and Executive

Provision/Points to Consider

1. **Term of Agreement of Employment**
    (a) Fixed nonrenewable term, *e.g.*, 2 or 3 years
    (b) Renewing term—"evergreen"
        (i) daily renewing until notice given
        (ii) renewing for successive 1- or 2-year periods if notice not given at least 1 year prior to end of initial term
    (c) Until attainment of specified age, *e.g.*, 62 or 65

2. **Position, Duties, Responsibilities, etc.**
    (a) Title/position
    (b) Seat on board of directors
    (c) Reporting relationship to board of directors or specified individual
    (d) Duties and responsibilities

(e) Work latitude
   (i)   service on outside boards
   (ii) charitable activities
   (iii) management of personal
         investments

3. **Salary**
   (a) Annual dollar amount
   (b) Annual review for increase or
       decrease by board
   (c) Use of COLAs
       (i) appropriate benchmark
   (d) Performance-related
   (e) Same percentage as average percentage
       increase awarded to executives reporting
       to Executive

4. **Bonus**
   (a) Sign-on bonus—"golden hello"
   (b) Fixed guaranteed amount—for how long
   (c) Stated percentage of salary
   (d) Discretionary with board
   (e) Performance-related—based on increase in
       (i)   return on equity
       (ii) achievement of certain stock price
       (iii) percentage of sales
       (iv) net earnings per share
       (v)   other
   (f) Opportunity to defer
       (i)   period of deferral
       (ii) rate of return on deferred amounts
       (iii) security arrangements for deferred
             bonus—"rabbi" or secular trust,
             surety bond, etc.

5. **Long-term Incentive**
    (a) Minimum—when paid?
    (b) Performance-related?
        (i) criteria, targets
    (c) Form of payment—cash and/or stock
    (d) Deferral opportunities—surety, etc.

6. **Equity Opportunity**
    (a) Type of opportunity
        (i) options—fair market value, below market or premium price
        (ii) restricted stock
        (iii) phantom stock
        (iv) stock appreciation rights
    (b) Discretionary or performance-related grants
        (i) within a plan
        (ii) outside a plan

7. **Employee Benefits and Perquisites**
    (a) Regular Company-sponsored plans
        (i) pension
        (ii) medical
        (iii) long-term disability
        (iv) travel accident and accidental death
        (v) term life
    (b) Supplemental plans
        (i) retirement—funded or unfunded, purchase of annuities, etc.
        (ii) long-term disability—insured or uninsured
        (iii) special executive medical
        (iv) life insurance, amount, type of policy, etc.
        (v) use of "portable," *i.e.*, individually owned benefits

8. **Perquisites**
   (a) Club memberships
   (b) Car and driver
   (c) Tax and financial counseling
   (d) Annual physical

9. **Termination of Employment/Consequences**

   A. Death
      (a) Continuation of salary—for what period?
      (b) Payment of partial bonus
      (c) Acceleration of stock options
      (d) Acceleration of long-term incentive
      (e) Continuation of special medical benefits for surviving spouse and children; if yes, for how long?

   B. Disability
      (a) Definition of "disability"
         (i) special definition
         (ii) definition in regular LTD plan
      (b) Continuation of salary—for what period
      (c) Payment of partial bonus
      (d) Acceleration of stock options
      (e) Acceleration of long-term incentive
      (f) Level of LTD benefits
         (i) 60%-65% of salary or salary *and* bonus
         (ii) insure or self-insure
      (g) Continuation of life insurance
      (h) Continuation of special medical benefits for spouse and children